The U.S. Naval Institute on
THE MARINE CORPS
AT WAR

U.S. NAVAL INSTITUTE
Chronicles

For nearly a century and a half since a group of concerned naval officers gathered to provide a forum for the exchange of constructive ideas, the U.S. Naval Institute has been a unique source of information relevant to the nation's sea services. Through the open forum provided by *Proceedings* and *Naval History* magazines, Naval Institute Press (the book-publishing arm of the institute), a robust Oral History program, and more recent immersion in various cyber activities (including the *Naval Institute Blog* and *Naval Institute News*), USNI has built a vast assemblage of intellectual content that has long supported the Navy, Marine Corps, and Coast Guard as well as the nation as a whole.

Recognizing the potential value of this exceptional collection, USNI has embarked on a number of new platforms to reintroduce readers to significant portions of this virtual treasure trove. The U.S. Naval Institute Chronicles series focuses on the relevance of history by resurrecting appropriate selections that are built around various themes, such as battles, personalities, and service components. Available in both paper and eBook versions, these carefully selected volumes help readers navigate through this intellectual labyrinth by providing some of the best contributions that have provided unique perspectives and helped shape naval thinking over the many decades since the institute's founding in 1873.

The U.S. Naval Institute on
THE MARINE CORPS AT WAR

THOMAS J. CUTLER
Series Editor

Naval Institute Press
Annapolis, Maryland

Naval Institute Press
291 Wood Road
Annapolis, MD 21402

Library of Congress Cataloging-in-Publication Data
Names: Cutler, Thomas J., date, editor of compilation. | United States Naval
    Institute, issuing body.
Title: The U.S. Naval Institute on the Marine Corps at war / Thomas J. Cutler.
Description: Annapolis, Maryland : Naval Institute Press, [2016] | Includes
    bibliographical references and index.
Identifiers: LCCN 2015051028| ISBN 9781682470428 (alk. paper) |
    ISBN 9781682470435 (mobi)
Subjects: LCSH: United States. Marine Corps—History.
Classification: LCC VE23 .U187 2016 | DDC 359.9/60973—dc23 LC
    record available at http://lccn.loc.gov/2015051028

♾ Print editions meet the requirements of ANSI/NISO z39.48–1992
(Permanence of Paper).
Printed in the United States of America.

24 23 22 21 20 19 18 17 16   9 8 7 6 5 4 3 2 1
First printing

CONTENTS

EDITOR'S NOTE

BECAUSE THIS BOOK is an anthology, containing documents from different time periods, the selections included here are subject to varying styles and conventions. Other variables are introduced by the evolving nature of the Naval Institute's publication practices. For those reasons, certain editorial decisions were required in order to avoid introducing confusion or inconsistencies and to expedite the process of assembling these sometimes disparate pieces.

Gender

Most jarring of the differences that readers will encounter are likely those associated with gender. A number of the included selections were written when the armed forces were primarily a male domain and so adhere to purely masculine references. I have chosen to leave the original language intact in these documents for the sake of authenticity and to avoid the complications that can arise when trying to make anachronistic adjustments. So readers are asked to "translate" (converting the ubiquitous "he" to "he or she" and "his" to "her or his" as required) and, while doing so, to celebrate the progress that we have made in these matters in more recent times.

Author "Biographies"

Another problem arises when considering biographical information of the various authors whose works make up this special collection. Some of the selections included in this anthology were originally accompanied by biographical information about their authors. Others were not. Those "biographies" that do exist have been included. They pertain to the time the article was written and may vary in terms of length and depth, some amounting to a single sentence pertaining to the author's current duty station, others consisting of several paragraphs that cover the author's career.

Ranks

I have retained the ranks of the authors *at the time of their publication*. As noted above, some of the authors wrote early in their careers, and the sagacity of their earlier contributions says much about the individuals, about the significance of the Naval Institute's forum, and about the importance of writing to the naval services—something that is sometimes underappreciated.

Other Anomalies

Readers may detect some inconsistencies in editorial style, reflecting staff changes at the Naval Institute, evolving practices in publishing itself, and various other factors not always identifiable. Some of the selections will include citational support, others will not. Authors sometimes coined their own words and occasionally violated traditional style conventions. *Bottom line:* with the exception of the removal of some extraneous materials (such as section numbers from book excerpts) and the conversion to a consistent font and overall design, these articles and excerpts appear as they originally did when first published.

ACKNOWLEDGMENTS

THIS PROJECT would not be possible without the dedication and remarkable industry of Denis Clift, the Naval Institute's vice president for planning and operations and president emeritus of the National Intelligence University. This former naval officer, who served in the administrations of eleven successive U.S. presidents and was once editor in chief of *Proceedings* magazine, bridged the gap between paper and electronics by single-handedly reviewing the massive body of the Naval Institute's intellectual content to find many of the treasures included in this anthology.

A great deal is also owed to Mary Ripley, Janis Jorgensen, Rebecca Smith, Judy Heise, Debbie Smith, Elaine Davy, and Heather Lancaster who devoted many hours and much talent to the digitization project that is at the heart of these anthologies.

Introduction

IN A 1925 U.S. NAVAL INSTITUTE *Proceedings* article, Major General John A. Lejeune, commandant of the Marine Corps, wrote that "the tenth day of November of this year will mark the one hundred fiftieth anniversary of the birth of the United States Marine Corps, since on November 10, 1775, the Continental Congress authorized the raising of two battalions of marines for the defense of the colonies which were then preparing to protect their rights, as they saw them, against the aggressions of the mother country." He went on to say that "from that distant date down to the present day the United States Marines have continued to serve as an integral part of the United States Navy and in peace and war have proved their worth as the military army of the Navy," adding that "in all of the wars in which the United States have engaged the marines have played their part according to their abilities and the occasions offered."

Those words serve as a reminder that the Marine Corps began as a component of the U.S. Navy. The evolution of warfare and of the Marines themselves has resulted in a degree of autonomy that makes the Corps a "service" in its own right. The commandant of Marines is a member of the Joint Chiefs of Staff and, more than once, a Marine general has served as chairman of that group. But as one reads through this anthology, one of the themes that emerges is that the Marine Corps remains a "*sea service*" with its ties to the Navy forming a symbiosis that is indisputable and essential to both, even if it is often masked by a healthy rivalry that results in biting but humorous comments, such as "the Marines see the Navy as a taxi service; the Navy sees Marines as cargo!"

In these selections from the U.S. Naval Institute's *Proceedings* and *Naval History* magazines, the eclectic history of the U.S. Marine Corps at war is presented as a collection of historical snapshots, ranging from the American Revolution to the twenty-first-century wars in Afghanistan and Iraq. The versatility of this unusual component of the nation's combat arms is made clear in these articles (and in the companion Chronicle *The U.S. Naval Institute on Marine Corps Aviation*), illustrating that Leathernecks have not only gone to sea with their Navy shipmates as originally intended, but have stormed ashore in great amphibious landings and have fought both guerillas and regulars in nearly every geographic realm, from the jungles of Central America to the mountains of Central Asia.

It is worthy to note that the U.S. Marine Corps has not only been unique and versatile but has maintained enviable standards of excellence throughout its long history. In that same 1925 article, General Lejeune noted that this exemplary Marine performance "is amply testified to in the many reports of the admirals who have commanded our squadrons and fleets on the seven seas." Few will dispute these sentiments expressed nearly a century ago, nor will there likely be many challenges to the general's concluding sentence: "The marines stand ready today to carry out their mission as an important part of the Navy and will continue to do all in their power to support the fleet, or any part thereof, in the accomplishment of [that] mission."

Semper Fi!

1

"American Marines in the Revolution"

Major Edwin N. McClellan, USMC

U.S. Naval Institute *Proceedings*
(June 1923): 957–63

"AT NO PERIOD OF THE NAVAL HISTORY of the world is it probable that Marines were more important than during the War of the Revolution," wrote J. Fenimore Cooper, and "the history of the Navy, even at that early day, as well as in these later times, abounds with instances of the gallantry and self-devotion of this body of soldiers."

The first blood of the American Revolution was shed at Lexington on April 19, 1775. After Ticonderoga had been captured, on May 10, there was difficulty in holding it, and men and money were asked for. It is in connection with the resulting relief expedition that American Marines are first mentioned in our history. In the expedition, so goes the account, were sent "500£ of money, escorted with eight Marines, well spirited and equipped." Arriving at Albany, additional troops joined the expedition, which soon arrived at Ticonderoga, after passing through territory infested by hostile Indians and treacherous renegades.

The earliest Marines, as also the earliest ships, belonged to the State Navies; before there were any ships in the Continental Navy, thousands of Marines served on the State vessels. Some were attached to the *Katy* and *Washington*, of the Rhode Island Navy, when, on June 15, 1775,

3

those warships chased ashore and destroyed an armed tender of the British Frigate *Rose*—the first enemy vessel captured by a public armed vessel during this war. The *Experiment*, launched on July 19, 1775, was the first vessel of the Pennsylvania Navy; South Carolina had vessels in commission by July 1775; Connecticut and Massachusetts by August, 1775; and Virginia by December 1775. The other States (except New Jersey and Delaware which had no Navies) acquired vessels on later dates.

Then on June 17 came Bunker Hill, and on July 3, George Washington assumed command of the Army around Boston. In addition, under orders of Congress he had "direction of the Naval Department" and well might be called the "Father of the American Navy."

On October 5, Congress directed General Washington to secure two armed vessels from Massachusetts, place them "on the Continental risqué and pay" and use them to capture two unescorted brigs loaded with munitions that had sailed from England. He was also instructed to give orders for the "proper encouragement to the Marines and Seamen" that served on the vessels. This was the first time the Continental Congress ever mentioned "Marines." Washington soon gathered together a fleet from the Navies of the New England States. The vessels were manned by crews, including Marines, taken, from his Army. Once on board, however, they belonged to the naval service, and in many instances there are references to the Marines serving on the *Hannah*, *Hancock*, *Lee*, *Lynch*, *Warren*, *Franklin*, *Harrison*, and *Washington*. The duty performed by these vessels had considerable effect in forcing the British to evacuate Boston on March 17, 1776 and thus the Marines shared in that success.

And so the American Marines of the State Navies and of Washington's Fleet, by their own acts, gradually established themselves in public favor. Congress became impressed with the fact that a corps of these Marines for the Continental Navy would be a fine thing.

There is a date that is celebrated every year by American Marines, wherever they are stationed throughout the world. It is November 10—the birthday of the Marine Corps. On that date, in 1775, Congress resolved: "That two Battalions of Marines be raised, consisting of one Colonel, two Lieutenant Colonels, two Majors, and other officers as usual in other regiments; and that they consist of an equal number of privates with other battalions; that particular care be taken, that no persons be appointed to office, or enlisted into said battalions, but such as are good seamen, or so acquainted with maritime affairs as to be able to serve to advantage by sea when required; that they be enlisted and commissioned to serve for and during the present war between Great Britain and the colonies, unless dismissed by order of Congress: that they be distinguished by the names of the first and second battalions of American Marines, and that they be considered as part of the number which the Continental Army before Boston is ordered to consist of." At first the enlistment period was for the war; later this was changed to include the period up to January 1, 1777, and after that the enlistment was for a stated term.

Washington received with dismay the orders to supply the personnel for this corps of Marines, and informed Congress that to supply them would "break through the whole system" in his Army which had "cost us so much time, anxiety, and pains, to bring into any tolerable form." This was because the Marines "must be acquainted with maritime affairs," wrote Washington, and because he would have to pick the Marines "out of the whole Army, one from this corps, one from another." He recommended that the Marines be raised in New York and Philadelphia. At last Washington stated that an "insuperable obstruction" consisted in the impossibility of getting the men to enlist for the "continuance of the war." On December 14, General Washington wrote Congress, "I am at a loss to know whether I am to raise the two battalions of Marines here or not." Again, on January 4, 1776, he wrote: "Congress will think me a little remiss, I fear, when I inform them that I have done nothing yet toward raising the battalion of Marines." Washington had ample excuse for this reluctance and procrastination; for he had twenty-six incomplete regiments at this time in his Army. His views evidently prevailed, for Congress soon directed that the Marines be raised from a source other than from his Army.

All this time, however, the Continental Marines had been in existence, and were working out their own salvation. The reluctance of George Washington to give up sufficient personnel from his Army for the organization of the two battalions had no retarding effect upon the appointment of officers or the enlisting of Marines.

As events turned out the colonel, the two lieutenant-colonels, one of the Majors, and the staff were not appointed. The highest ranking officer of Marines serving during the Revolution was Major Samuel Nicholas, who after active service with Hopkins' Fleet, and in the Battles of Trenton and Princeton, performed duties at the Capital that corresponded more or less to those of the commandant today; and in addition acted, at one time, as muster master for the Navy.

The "First and Second Battalions of American Marines" were never actually organized and named as such. When the emergency or demand for the use of Marines arose, provisional units, from a squad to a battalion, were organized. When a vessel of the Navy went into commission a Marine Guard was formed and marched on board. When the object for which the provisional unit was organized had been accomplished, or a vessel no longer required a Marine Guard, the unit was disbanded and the officers and men used for other purposes.

These, however, were not the only Continental Marines. There were those who were appointed and enlisted in Europe, for the vessels of John Paul Jones' squadron, and other ships such as the *Boston*. Many of these Marines were French, and of other nationalities. In addition to these Continental or Federal Marines, there were the thousands serving on the privateers, who were sometimes called "Gentlemen Sailors" or "Gentlemen Volunteers." There were also those who were attached to vessels of the State Navies. And there were those who were detailed, from the Army, to act as Marines on particular occasions.

Marine officers received the same character of commissions as did the Army and Navy officers. Samuel Nicholas was the "oldest officer of Marines." He "entered into the service in the capacity of a Captain of Marines" (being commissioned as such on November 28, 1775) and probably received the first commission in the Continental naval service, known of today.

The methods and plans of recruiting Marines were very little different from those used today. Offers of prize-money, advance money, expense money, bounty money, pensions, and promises of ample grog rations were the lures presented to those who were in a "recruiting mood." Handbills were used extensively to make public the recruiting propaganda. Attractively uniformed recruiting parties, preceded by drum, fife, and colors, noised their way up and down the streets of the cities and large towns and ended up at a rendezvous with a queue of patriots who thus early obeyed the command to "Join the Marines."

Benjamin Franklin wrote that in 1775 he had observed in Philadelphia on one of the drums belonging to the Marines—whose recruiters were raising two battalions—"there was painted the rattlesnake with this motto under it, 'Don't tread on me!'" He said, knowing it was the custom to have some device on the Arms of every country, that he supposed this design was intended for the Arms of North America. It is claimed by many that this device of the Marines was on the first flag that flew from the mastheads of our first ships of war.

Philadelphia was the leading Marine Corps recruiting city of the United States, and probably the most famous of all recruiting rendezvous established during the Revolution was that located in the Tun Tavern in Philadelphia. This was a once prominent hostelry on the east side of King (Water) Street, at the corner of a small thoroughfare known as Wilcox's (later as Tun) Alley, that led down to the Delaware River. Captain Robert Mullen, proprietor of the tavern, was captain of a company of Marines.

Marine officers were also used extensively for recruiting personnel for the Navy. For example, Captains Matthew Parke, Edward Arrowsmith and Second Lieutenant Samuel Wallingford of the Marines, under the direction of John Paul Jones, assisted in recruiting the crew of the *Ranger* in the late summer of 1777; and the crew of the *Providence* at Plymouth, Mass., in 1776, was another instance.

Marines performed all sorts of duty. With necessary officers they were detached for service on board the armed vessels of the United States, and thus engaged in every important battle afloat; participated in important landing parties from naval vessels, such as the one at New Providence (Bahamas) in 1776; at Whitehaven (England); at St. Mary's Isle (Kirkcudbright, Scotland); and again at New Providence in 1778; were ordered to do duty in forts, such as Fort Montgomery in New York; performed expeditionary duty, such as the Penobscot Expedition in 1779, and the expedition down the Mississippi to the Gulf of Mexico on the *Rattletrap* at an earlier date; were detached for service with the Army during the period when they fought at Trenton and Princeton; performed artillery duty with the Army; guarded enemy prisoners; acted as guards at naval stations ashore; went to the Indian-infested forests of Pennsylvania, and brought out masts for the frigates of the Navy; and acted as officer-couriers and Continental Express Riders in America and Europe.

The principal duty, of course, was service on board the ships of the Navy. The strength of the Marine Guards varied considerably. The thumb rule which determined the strength was that there should be one Marine for each gun on the ship, but this rule had many exceptions. The frigates carried about sixty Marines but the duties expected of the various ships frequently caused a considerable increase in the strength of the Marine Guard. Boarding and repelling boarders and the close range at which naval battles were fought made the musketry fire of the Marines an important element of combat.

On board the Privateers, the Marine was a very high type of man and fighting was his only duty. When the United States Schooner *Revenge* was captured and later laid up at Portsmouth Prison in England, one of the "Gentlemen Sailors" of that vessel was discovered to be a woman.

The duties of the Marines on board ship consisted of sentry duty at important posts throughout the ship, and during action, they were often stationed in the tops, where the expert shots were of great assistance. Cooper wrote that the Marines were "strictly infantry soldiers" who were "trained to serve afloat; and their discipline, equipments, spirit, character, and esprit de corps are altogether those of an Army. The Marines impart to a ship of war, in a great degree, its high military character. They furnish all the guards and sentinels; in battle they repel, or cover the assaults of boarders; and at all times they sustain and protect the stem and necessary discipline of a ship by their organization, distinctive character, training, and we might add, nature." While the Marines at times manned the great guns, "their proper weapons" were "the musket and bayonet."

Green was the dominant color of the Continental Marines' uniform during the Revolution. An officer wore a green coat with white facings and skirts turned back. The coat had slashed sleeves and pockets and had buttons around the cuffs. A silver epaulette was worn on the right shoulder. The waistcoat was of white material. The breeches were white, edged with green. Black gaiters and garters were part of the uniform. The buttons were of silver and carried a foul anchor. A sword and other necessary equipment were carried.

The "regimentals" of the enlisted man consisted of a green coat faced with red, a green shirt, a white woolen jacket, light colored cloth breeches, woolen stockings, and a round hat with white binding. His buttons were of pewter and carried a foul anchor. While in European waters, John Paul Jones dressed his Marines in the English uniform—red and white, instead of the green as prescribed by the Marine Committee. The Marines of each State Navy also wore distinctive uniforms.

Congress prescribed the rates of pay for the officers while the pay of the enlisted men was the same as the Army. A captain of Marines received thirty dollars a month; a lieutenant twenty dollars; sergeants eight dollars; the corporals, drummers and fifers, seven dollars and one-third; and the privates six dollars and two-thirds.

Congress carefully prescribed that the Marines would share equally in all prize money and accorded them the same rights with regard to pensions as provided for the Army and Navy. The Marines of the State Navies were also treated generously in regard to pay, prize-money, and pensions.

At the termination of the struggle the Marine Corps, like the Army and Navy, was disbanded, "literally leaving nothing behind it," as J. Fenimore Cooper most appropriately stated, "but the recollections of its services and sufferings."

"River Raid on Korea"

2

Lieutenant Colonel Merrill L. Bartlett,
USMC (Ret.), and Jack Sweetman

Naval History (December 2001): 43–47

IN AN EXCERPT from the new Naval Institute Press book, The U.S. Marine Corps: An Illustrated History, *the authors recount the Korean Expedition of 1871—a military success but a diplomatic failure.*

The largest-scale combat in which Leathernecks participated in the three decades following the Civil War was the Korean Expedition of 1871. On 23 May of that year, five vessels of Rear Admiral John Rodgers's Asiatic Fleet—the frigate *Colorado*, sloops *Alaska* and *Benicia*, and gunboats *Monocacy* and *Palos*—entered Roze Roads on the west coast of Korea not far from Chemulpo (modern-day Inchon). Aboard Admiral Rodgers's flagship, the *Colorado*, was Frederick F. Low, the U.S. minister to China, who had been sent to open diplomatic relations with the hermit kingdom of Korea. Contact was made with the local inhabitants, and on the 31st a small delegation of third- and fifth-rank Korean officials appeared. Low refused to receive them, directing his secretary to explain that the presence of first-rank officials qualified to conduct negotiations was required. In the meantime, the Koreans were informed, the Americans desired to chart the Salee River, as the channel of the Han River between Kanghwa-do (island) and the Kumpo Peninsula was then called.

11

As the Han leads to the capital city of Seoul, the Koreans might have been expected to consider such an act provocative, American assurances of goodwill notwithstanding, but they raised no objections. Twenty-four hours were allotted for them to notify the appropriate authorities.

Accordingly, at noon on 1 June, four steam launches followed by the *Monocacy* and *Palos* set out to begin the survey. As they came abreast of the fortifications on the heights of Kanghwa-do, the Koreans opened fire. The surveying party replied with gusto, shelling the forts into silence, and returned to the fleet's anchorage. American casualties were two men wounded.

Admiral Rodgers waited nine days for an apology or better tides. The former was not forthcoming, and on 10 June a punitive expedition entered the river with the mission of capturing and destroying the errant forts. The landing force numbered 686 officers and men, including 109 Marines organized into two little companies and a naval battery of seven 12-pounder howitzers. Fire support would be provided by the gunboats and four steam launches mounting 12-pounders in their bows. Commander L. A. Kimberly was placed in command of the landing force; Captain McLane Tilton led its Leathernecks. Tilton was one of those unconventional characters for whom the Corps has always seemed to exercise an attraction. (Writing his wife from a Mediterranean deployment, he reported that when he first went on deck each day, "If anyone asks me how are you old fellow, I reply, 'I don't feel very well; no gentleman is ever well in the morning.'")

Three forts, each with a walled water-battery, overlooked the shore of Kanghwa-do. In the course of the operation, the Americans christened them the Marine Redoubt, Fort Monocacy, and The Citadel. The Monocacy took the first two under fire shortly after noon. Both had been silenced by the time the *Palos* appeared with the landing party's boats in tow about an hour later. The boats cast off half a mile below the nearest fort, and at 1345 that afternoon the Bluejackets and Marines began struggling ashore across a broad, knee-deep mudflat "crossed by deep sluices," a disgusted Tilton noted, "filled with softer and still deeper mud." Some men left their shoes, socks, leggings, and even trouser legs behind, and the howitzers bogged down to their barrels. Fortunately, the Koreans did not attempt to oppose the landing.

The Leathernecks had been selected to serve as the expedition's advance guard. Tilton deployed them into a skirmish line as soon as they left the boats. Once both companies reached firm ground, Commander Kimberly ordered Tilton to lead his Marines toward the fort, an elliptical stone redoubt with 12-foot walls. Most of the sailors remained behind to manhandle the guns out of the muck. On the Marines' approach, the fort's white-robed defenders fled, firing a few parting shots. The work mounted 54 guns, but all except two were insignificant brass breechloaders. Tilton halted his men until the main body came up, "when we were again ordered to push forward," he wrote, "which we did, scouring the fields as far as practicable from the left of the line of march, the river being on our right, and took a position on a wooded knoll . . . commanding a fine view of the beautiful hills and inundated rice fields immediately around us." At this point he received orders to hold for the night. It was 1630 before the guns had been dragged ashore, and too few hours of daylight remained to demolish the captured fort and tackle the next. The seamen bivouacked half a mile to the rear.

The landing force moved out at 0530 the next morning. Its fire support had been reduced by the withdrawal of the *Palos*, which had hurt herself on an uncharted rock while the landing was in progress, but that available from the *Monocacy* and the launches would prove more than sufficient. The second fort, a chipped granite structure about 90 feet square, stood on a bluff a mile upstream. Tilton's men found it deserted. While a Marine bugler amused himself by rolling 33 little brass cannon over the bluff into the river, other members of the expedition spiked the fort's four big guns and tore down two of its walls. The march was then resumed.

The track between the first two forts had been relatively easy going, but beyond the second it became extremely difficult, "the topography of the country being indescribable," Tilton reported, "resembling a sort of 'chopped sea' of immense hills and deep ravines lying in every conceivable position." Presently the column came under long-range musket fire from a Korean force estimated to number from 2,000 to 5,000 among some hills beyond the Americans' left flank. Five guns supported by three companies of seamen were deployed to hold this body in check, and the remainder of the party continued its advance. On two occasions the Koreans made a rush toward the detachment, but a few artillery shells turned them back each time.

The last and strongest of the Korean fortifications, The Citadel, was a stone redoubt crowning a steep, conical hill on a peninsula some two miles upstream from its neighbor. The *Monocacy* and the steam launches opened fire on the Citadel at about 1100. At noon, Commander Kimberly halted his command 600 yards from the fort to give the men a breather. By that time, the parties of Koreans seen falling back on The Citadel and the forest of flags in and around it left no doubt that the position would be defended.

After signaling the *Monocacy* to cease fire, the storming party, 350 seamen and Marines with fixed bayonets, dashed forward to occupy a ridgeline only 120 yards from the fort. Although Tilton's men were still armed with the model 1861 muzzle-loading Springfield rifle musket (in his words "a blasted old 'Muzzle-Fuzzel'"), they quickly established fire superiority over the fort's defenders, who were armed with matchlocks, a firearm that had disappeared from Western arsenals 200 years before. "The firing continued for only a few minutes, say four," Tilton wrote, "amidst the melancholy songs of the enemy, their bearing being courageous in the extreme."

At 1230 Lieutenant Commander Silas Casey, commanding the Blue-jacket battalion, gave the order to charge. "[A]nd as little parties of our forces advanced closer and closer down the deep ravine between us,"

Tilton continued, "some of [the Koreans] mounted the parapet and threw stones etc., at us, uttering the while exclamations seemingly of defiance." The first American into The Citadel, Navy Lieutenant Hugh W. McKee, fell mortally wounded by a musket ball in the groin and a spear thrust in the side. The spearman also stabbed at Lieutenant Commander Winfield Scott Schley, who had followed close behind McKee. The point passed between Schley's left arm and his chest, pinning his sleeve to his coat, and he shot the man dead.

Tilton was among half a dozen officers who led their men into the fort moments later. The Koreans stood their ground, and the fighting became hand to hand. Clambering over the parapet, Private Michael McNamara encountered an enemy soldier pointing a matchlock at him. He wrenched the gun from the Korean's hands and clubbed him to death with it. Private James Dougherty closed with and killed the man the Americans identified as the commander of the Korean forces. Tilton, Private Hugh Purvis, and Corporal Charles Brown converged on The Citadel's principal standard, a 12-foot-square yellow cotton banner emblazoned with black characters signifying "commanding general." For five minutes the fort's interior was a scene of desperate combat. Then the remaining defenders fled downhill toward the river, under fire from the Marines, a company of seamen, and the two howitzers that had accompanied the attackers.

A total of 143 Korean dead and wounded were counted in and around the Citadel, and Lieutenant Commander Schley, the landing force's adjutant, estimated that another 100 had been killed in flight. Forty-seven flags and 481 pieces of ordnance, most quite small but including 27 sizable pieces—20-pounders and upward—were captured. The storming party lost three men killed and ten wounded, with a Marine private in each category. Captain Tilton was pleasantly surprised by his survival. In a letter home a few days later, he wrote, "I never expected to see my wife and baby any more, and if it hadn't been that the Coreans [sic] can't shoot true, I never should." He retired as a lieutenant colonel in

1897. Nine sailors and six Marines were awarded the Medal of Honor. Among the latter were Corporal Brown and Private Purvis, who had rendezvoused with Tilton at the Citadel's flagstaff.

The landing force reembarked early the next morning, leaving The Citadel in ruins. "Thus," wrote Admiral Rodgers, "was a treacherous attack upon our people and an insult to our flag redressed." Successful as it had been from a military standpoint, however, the operation was not a masterstroke of diplomacy. Subsequent communications with Korean authorities, conducted by messages tied to a pole on an island near the anchorage, were entirely unproductive, and on 3 July the fleet withdrew. A treaty with Korea was not negotiated until 1882.

Lieutenant Colonel Bartlett has written, edited, and collaborated on seven books and has won the Robert D. Heinl Jr. Award twice for articles published in the U.S. Naval Institute *Proceedings*. A two-tour veteran of the Vietnam War, he earned a Navy Commendation Medal with Combat V and a Vietnamese Cross of Gallantry with Silver Star. He also earned the William P. Clements Award as outstanding military instructor during his tenure teaching history at the U.S. Naval Academy.

Dr. Sweetman taught history at the U.S. Naval Academy for 20 years. He is the author, editor, or translator of numerous Naval Institute Press books and is consulting editor of *Naval History*. He has received the *Naval History* Author of the Year Award, the U.S. Navy League's Alfred Thayer Mahan Award for Literary Achievement, and the North American Society for Oceanic History's John Lyman Book Award. Recently, he was elected to be a Fellow of the Royal Historical Society.

3 "The Marines at Playa Del Este"

Carlos C. Hanks

U.S. Naval Institute *Proceedings*
(November 1941): 1591–93

WHEN ADMIRAL CERVERA'S SQUADRON had been trapped in the harbor of Santiago, the American fleet settled down to a grim and unwearied blockade, thereby beginning a new naval phase of the Spanish-American War, with new problems to be met and new plans to meet any exigency.

One problem confronting Admiral Sampson was the establishment of a base not too far away where his ships could be coaled and minor repairs effected. An ideal location for such a base was Guantanamo Bay, only about 60 miles to the eastward of Santiago.

On June 7, 1898, the small, unprotected cruiser *Marblehead*, Commander Bowman McCalla, U.S. Navy, reconnoitered the bay in company with the auxiliary cruisers *Yankee* and *St. Louis*, and drove the little Spanish gunboat *Sandoval* into the shoal waters of the inner harbor, quite out of range of the deep draft ships.

While the *St. Louis* was cutting the cable, a detachment of marines comprising the cruiser *New York*'s marine guard, 40 from the battleship *Oregon* and 20 from the *Marblehead*, landed from the cruiser under the command of Captain M. C. Goodrell, U.S. Marine Corps, of the *New*

York. The landing party burned the few huts at Playa del Este, destroyed the cable station at the mouth of the bay, and hunted vainly for Spanish soldiers who had scattered under the preliminary shelling by the ships. The marines re-embarked and the *Yankee* departed with the *New York* and *Oregon* contingents, leaving the *Marblehead* to watch the bay alone for the next three days. Then on June 10 the naval transport *Panther* arrived with the dispatch boat *Dolphin* in company.

The *Panther* had on board 23 officers of the Marine Corps, a naval surgeon, and 623 marine enlisted men, all under the command of Lieutenant Colonel Robert W. Huntington, U.S. Marine Corps, who had instructions to land and establish a base for the fleet.

Thus, while Admiral Sampson lay off Santiago holding Cervera a prisoner and awaiting the arrival of the Army, the first actual invasion of Cuba by United States forces began at Guantanamo Bay. The marines filled whaleboats and cutters and were towed to the beach by steam launches. They landed with precision, and in less than an hour the entire battalion was ashore with its tents and supplies.

Climbing a hill that rose sharply from the beach, the battalion reached the summit without opposition, finding itself on a plateau several acres in size and dotted with woods and chaparral. Soon, tents appeared in trim rows, while parties were sent out to clear the brush about the camp, a job that proved almost hopeless with the appliances at hand.

The battalion settled down for the night without seeing a single Spaniard. But darkness brought the enemy and guerrillas began popping at the outposts, killing two privates, James McColgan and William Dumphy, and preventing the weary marines from obtaining sleep. The *Marblehead* and *Dolphin* shelled the surrounding countryside but were unable to dislodge the Spaniards from cover. Assistant Surgeon John Blair Gibbs, U.S. Navy, was killed in front of his tent, and Sergeant C. H. Smith was shot dead in the front lines before daylight came. The night's toll also included several men wounded.

The Spaniards continued to harass the marines, laboring to deepen their shallow rifle pits, and on the morning of the 12th Sergeant Major Henry Good was killed. That day a force of 60 Cubans, commanded by Lieutenant Colonel Thomas, joined the marines. Colonel Huntington said of these: "They, being acquainted with the country and excellent woodsmen and fearless, were of the greatest assistance."

The marines were under steady rifle fire from the brush and the morning of the 14th brought the sixth death to the command, when Private Goode Taurman fell off a cliff and was killed. The wounded had reached a total of 22.

With his men worn out from lack of sleep and growing steadily more irritable under the annoyance of the guerrilla peppering, Colonel Huntington assumed the offensive on the 14th. He sent Companies C and D, with the 60 Cubans, to destroy a well about 6 miles from camp. This well was said to be the only Spanish water supply within 9 miles, and without it the Spaniards would be compelled to retire to Caimanera, a small garrison town about 10 miles from the bay proper and thus out of reach of the ships.

Another force of Spaniards, more numerous than the marines, was located around Playa del Este, on the eastern arm of the harbor. This force remained discreetly inactive after discovering that Commander McCalla's ships were quite ready to shell the shore, given the slightest excuse.

The well-taking expedition, 211 men in all, with Captain G. F. Elliott, senior officer of the marines, left camp under the command of the Cuban Lieutenant Colonel Thomas and was soon mixed up in a hot little scrap with some 500 Spaniards that lasted from about 11:00 A.M. until nearly 3:00 P.M.

They fought over the ridges and through brush-choked valleys until the Spaniards finally fled in disorder, leaving 60 dead including two officers. A lieutenant and 17 privates were captured by the Americans. Three marines were wounded, while the Cubans had two killed and two wounded.

Captain Elliott's report particularly commended First Lieutenant W. C. Neville, who injured a hip and an ankle in a fall after the fight was over; First Lieutenant L. C. Lucas, commanding Company C; Captain William F. Spicer, commanding Company D; Second Lieutenants L. J. Magill, P. M. Bannon and M. J. Shaw; Sergeant John H. Quick, who constantly exposed himself to enemy fire while signaling to the *Dolphin*, and Privates Faulkner, Boniface, and Carter for unusually deadly marksmanship.

The report cites the effectiveness of shellfire from the *Dolphin*, Commander H. W. Lyon, and the care that ship gave 12 marines, including Captain Spicer, who were overcome by the heat and sent out to her for treatment.

This fight, in which Captain Elliott also distinguished himself, brought an end to Spanish action against the marine battalion, and no further sniping occurred, although vigilance was maintained to guard against a surprise attack.

Relieved of enemy pressure, the marines strengthened their position while bluejackets landed stores, rebuilt the cable house, and spliced the cut cable, giving the Navy its own communication channel.

With this work in hand, Admiral Sampson sent the battleship *Texas* and the *Suwanee*, an armed lighthouse tender, to shell a small fort on the western arm of the harbor, the opposite side to the location of the marine camp. Occasional firing had come from this fort, and it was necessary to drive all the enemy from the area and back to Caimanera if the bay was to be entirely safe for the coaling and repair of ships.

The fort could provide little resistance, but an element of danger entered into the attack through the presence of submarine mines in the western channel. The fort was destroyed by the two ships with the assistance of the *Marblehead* which picked up a contact mine on her propeller. The *Texas* also knocked one adrift, but, by good fortune, neither exploded.

With the last enemy work reduced, Sampson's ships began regular coaling at Guantanamo, and they lay there untroubled to effect repairs when necessary. The water was deep enough for battleships, the climate was reasonably healthy, and no Spaniards appeared to mar the calm. The latter remained at Caimanera, and the little gunboat *Sandoval* also went up to that town, well out of range.

Steam launches kept the channel swept in case the Spaniards set mines adrift, and maintained a constant patrol against a possible torpedo attack by the *Sandoval*. But no attack ever came and the launch crews had only occasional opportunities to fire their little one-pounders at the distant gunboat, as their one relief from the monotony of their vigil.

On the 18th, Admiral Sampson, in his flagship *New York*, made his first visit to his squadron's new base and found everything in excellent order. The marines were comfortable and healthy on shore—in fact not one death occurred through sickness during the entire marine occupation of Playa del Este. In the bay, the battleship *Iowa* and auxiliary cruiser *Yankee* lay peacefully coaling, while riding at anchor were the *Marblehead, Dolphin, Panther*, the hospital ship *Solace*, the lighthouse tender *Armeria*, and three colliers.

Probably nothing in the entire naval campaign against the Spanish forces in Cuba brought more credit to the acumen of Admiral Sampson than the acquisition of Guantanamo Bay, nor can the work done by the small force of marines in a strange country, confronted by enemies fully three times as numerous and well hidden by luxuriant undergrowth, be too highly praised. It was a model campaign and one described by no less an authority than the military expert of the London *Standard*, as a "master stroke."

4 *"The* Marine Brigade"

Captain John W. Thomason Jr., USMC

U.S. Naval Institute *Proceedings*
(November 1928): 963–68

THE WAR WITH GERMANY was an anonymous sort of war, fought obscurely by unnamed battalions behind a veil of censorship. In other wars, the patriotic citizenry back home, eating corn bread and enduring meatless days, might find spice for such unexciting rations in the dispatches from the front. In Rome, the plebs around the bulletin boards learned with cheers of the smart conduct of the 10th Legion, which, taken in a narrow place by swarming Gauls, rallied to the personal appeal of Caesar, broke the enemy and drove him. Paris of the Consulate was informed by the fastest post of the fortitude of the 52nd Demi-Brigade (Seine-et-Marne); it formed front to a flank under Austrian fire, and struck terribly across the bridge at Lodi; General Buonaparte considered that the 52nd Demi-Brigade (Seine-et-Marne) deserved well of the Fatherland. Englishmen drank themselves blind to the Foot Guards who held Hugomont against the battering of Ney on the flank at Waterloo, and to the 92nd Highlanders who charged, clinging to the stirrups of the Scots Greys, until the cuirassiers of Milhaud and Lobau cut them down. There are men alive today who read the flashes from Gettysburg, of the Iron Brigade of Wisconsin at Culp's Hill by Gettysburg, and of Pickett's

Division that attacked on the third day in the center. Most of us remember headlines: the Rough Riders at San Juan Hill. But in our last war, the hands of the correspondents were held where their eyes were not hooded. Mr. Forbes would never have gotten the story of Balaklava past the censors, nor would Alfred, Lord Tennyson have been allowed to publish "The Charge of the Light Brigade."

In the American Expeditionary Forces there was one unit, and only one, while the Germans still held out, whose name got through the fog. This was the Brigade of Marines in the 2nd Division, U.S. Regular. The story involves certain war correspondents, so charged with suppressed news that they were near to bursting, and a chief of censors, honest and able and anxious to accommodate, but perhaps a little clouded in his mind as to what marines were, and why—a condition not ever uncommon in the Army; and for two thrilling days the press of the nation clanged with the doings of 7,500 leathernecks at a place called Belleau Woods, while numerous infantry brigades, earnest and meritorious, sweated in silence, and continued so to toil.

A little later, when calmness descended, and the instructed press was making what it could out of such sterile items as, "Yesterday the American 1st Army Corps made some progress towards the Vesle," people asked: How come these marines, anyway? We thought the Army fought on land—it did, and does. But about that Marine Brigade. . . .

Major General George Barnett was commandant of the Marine Corps. Stirred by small enterprises at Vera Cruz, in Santo Domingo, and in Haiti, the marine recruiting service had evolved the slogan, "First to Fight." Headquarters read the writing on the wall, and Headquarters realized that the marines must get into the German War or become quite ridiculous—all this aside from the sound necessity of giving marine officers experience in large operations ashore. Very early in 1917, the major general commandant had a concentration of veteran marines at Philadelphia, and others within reach. When the United States declared war

against the Germans, General Barnett was able, with the fullest coöpera-
tion from Mr. Secretary Daniels, to offer to the President for service with
the Army, a war-strength regiment of marines, assembled and drilling in
battalions, and ready to go.

At that time, the Army was hard put to it for trained soldiers. The
old regular regiments were being split into three; you had one old regiment, much diluted, and two new ones. The draft was in the air and the
National Guard was recruiting up to strength. The Secretary of War was
pleased to accept the proffered regiment of marines: he promised that it
would sail with the very first Army contingent.

But when that contingent was made up—the infantry units which
became the American 1st Division—in June of 1917, the Navy was
advised that, most unfortunately, no transportation for marines existed.
They would surely go in the next convoy sailing. The commandant of
marines had this in a personal note from Mr. Secretary Baker, and he
took it to Mr. Secretary Daniels. And General Barnett relates that it was
the proudest moment in all his long career, when he informed the Secretary of War that the Army need give itself no distress about sailing
accommodations for marines: he had the *Henderson*, and the *De Kalb*,
and the *Von Steuben*—ex-German liners, the last two—and the Navy
would see its own marines to France.

So the 5th Regiment of Marines, Colonel Doyen, sailed in the first
convoy, trained for a while in France with the 1st Division, General Sib-
ert, and was then split up variously on military police and construction
details, laying the ground work for the A.E.F.

In the meantime, on September 20, 1917, the War Department
approved the organization of a unit to be designated as the American 2nd
Division, U.S. Regular. To it were posted the 2nd Field Artillery Brigade,
the 2nd Engineers, various auxiliaries, and the 3rd Brigade of Infantry,
which last was made up of the 9th and 23rd Infantry Regiments. The
other infantry brigade would be formed by the major general commandant of marines, and would be known as the 4th Brigade. General Barnett

had his second regiment of marines ready: it was formed at Quantico. The 5th Regiment had been largely veteran; old-timers with all the campaign ribbons and rows of hash marks. The new regiment, the 6th, had a seasoning of trained men, but its ranks were filled with volunteers, from college graduates to ditchdiggers. In the fall and winter of 1917 it crossed to France, and with it the nucleus of the 6th Machine Gun Battalion, Colonel Catlin commanding the 6th Marines, and Major Cole, the machine guns.

In October, 1917, the 2nd Division was directed to its designated training area in France. All its regiments were much scattered, and although General Bundy of the Army had been detailed to command, its first orders were signed by Brigadier General Doyen, of the marines, newly promoted, and senior officer present. Through the winter of 1917–18, the division assembled, coming in by battalions and companies from the jobs on which it had been dispersed. A detachment of the 5th Regiment went as far afield as Southampton, England, policing Army rest camps in that vicinity. It was February, 1918, before all the infantry of the division was together; it was March before the artillery joined, and not until May were all its elements brought under the division command. About the middle of March the 2nd Division went up to the front, taking over sectors of the Toulon-Rupt-Troyon line, between Verdun and St. Mihiel. Two American divisions, the 1st and the 26th, were on the front before it. Of all the American regular divisions, the training of the 2nd was the most haphazard and sketchy, and its assembly the most delayed. It got many of its officers and some of its "non-coms" to the service schools before it went into the line, but actually, it learned its business under fire.

From the point where the division entered the line, in that bleak, wet March of 1918, to the day in August of the next year when the marines took train for Quantico, after the parade in New York, it is very hard to set forth a separate history of the Marine Brigade, which was the 5th Regiment and the 6th Regiment and the 6th Machine Gun Battalion, and officers and men of the Navy medical corps. Its first commanding officer was General Doyen of the Marine Corps; his health failing, General Harbord of the Army relieved him. After June, 1918, it had a marine brigadier, General Neville; after Soissons, in July, the 2nd Division was commanded by a marine, General Lejeune. But its history is the history of the American 2nd Division, and they all—four regiments of infantry, three machine gun battalions, three regiments of artillery, the engineers, the signal troops, and the trains—write the same names on their battle flags.

Divisions, like regiments and companies and ships and persons, have individuality. The 1st Division, for example, the most thoroughly trained and the oldest of the A.E.F. units, was methodical, tenacious, and steady in all its fighting. It did not move quickly; its blows were calculated and powerful and sustained. The 2nd Division was characterized by the quality of dash. No troops in any war ever reorganized more quickly, given a breathing space, than the Germans. If you stopped to bring up your services, and to adjust your communications, Heinie was at you with a counterattack. But if you hit him and kept on hitting, he tended to disintegrate. There are three great attacks in the annals of the 2nd Division: the attack of July 18, that broke through the Forest de Retz, rolled over Chaudun and Vierzy, and stopped within rifle shot of the vital Soissons—Château-Thierry road; the attack of October 3, that overwhelmed Blanc Mont Ridge in the Champagne so swiftly that German observers were captured in their towers, and all the German defense system to right and left paralyzed until too late to recover anything; and the strange thrust of the night of November 4, when the 3rd Brigade seized a narrow bit of German front and marched in column by a wood road, through the rainy dark, from La Nouart to Tuillerie Farm, disrupting a German corps and seizing the Beaumont ridge, so that the German organization crumbled on the whole corps front, and the Germans fled across the Meuse. All these had a terrifying swiftness about them. And I think that the secret lies in the mixed character of the 2nd Division. United against everything outside the division, there was within it a fierce rivalry between the marines and the infantry. Looking over to the left, where the marine battalions also lay under hells of shelling, the doughboys of the 3rd Brigade considered that they could stand anything them dam' leathernecks could. Working forward under the scourge of machine-gun fire, marines of all ranks were goaded by the fear that them Army files might get ahead of them—Come on, you birds! And the careful records of German divisions attest the savage energy of these attacks; as attest also the battle maps that show advances day by day; and the casualty lists. The 2nd Division had more casualties than any other American division; in captures of prisoners and guns only the 1st Division approached it.

Napoleon rated high among the military qualities essential to success, luck. The Marine Brigade was lucky. The pure chance of battle brought it the opportunity which lifted it briefly from the anonymity of this war. Luck can do no more for any man or any brigade than bring opportunity; after that it is a matter of training, of discipline, of skill. I do not think these facts have been before set down.

At the end of May, 1918, the 2nd Division lay in the area Chaumont-en-Vexen, which is north and a little west of Paris, as you go towards Rouen, and more than a hundred kilometers from Château-Thierry. The division was to go to the area Beauvais, behind Cantigny, where the 1st Division had had an adventure, taken some mauling, and captured a town, and was due for a relief. The drive of the German 7th Army, down from the Chemin des Dames, between Reims and Soissons, to the Marne at Château-Thierry, upset these plans. The 2nd Division was ordered to the French 6th Army, then broken into pieces by the impact of von Boehn's shock divisions, and fighting desperately in the Château-Thierry area to restore the front. The division was moved by camions on the last day of May to the area Montreuil, as you go to Château-Thierry from Meaux; the infantry regiments debussed during the afternoon and night of May 31, near the town May-en-Multien, and marched towards the front. The fog of war existed very terribly on this front, that day. The French 21st Corps, General Degoutte, did not know where the front was, for the front was moving very fast, or where its own divisions were, for they were fighting bitter rear-guard actions, by companies and battalions, and being destroyed; and the German 4th Reserve Corps, having taken Château-Thierry, was swinging westward in an orderly advance, rolling up the broken French elements. Consequently, between four o'clock in the afternoon of May 31 and midnight, May 31/June 1, the 2nd Division received four sets of orders from the French corps and army command, each set locating it in a different area, as the situation changed in the eyes of French Headquarters. The last order deployed it in the area Montreuil, between that place and Château-Thierry, astride the great Paris-Metz highway. The 2nd Division issued its own orders on this basis, locating the 3rd Brigade of Infantry to the north of the road, where it would have faced the Bois de Belleau and Hill 142 and Bouresches, and the 4th Brigade of Marines to the south, in front of Hill 204 and Vaux.

Meantime, the 9th Infantry, having marched all night with its colonel on foot at its head, came upon the Paris-Metz road soon after sunrise, June 1. The Germans were then mounting Hill 204, and to the French corps command the more immediate menace seemed from the east, from the direction of the hill. The 9th Infantry was deployed to meet it, and formed line south of the highway. The next regiment to arrive was the 6th Marines, in the afternoon. The Germans were appearing on the high ground north of the road, and the marines went into line behind the French then fighting in that direction. On these two movements, dictated by the emergency of the moment, the division line built up during the succeeding days, the 5th Marines going in on the left of the 6th Marines, and the 23rd Infantry with the 9th. Later, when the situation began to stabilize, the French corps commander considered it necessary to improve his left front, and this called for the reduction of the towns of Veuilly and Bussiares and Bouresches, and the Bois de Belleau, the last two points named being on the front of the Marine Brigade. The marines and the French 167th Division, on their left, were at this task for the rest of June, and accomplished it. The regulars of the 3rd Brigade did not have their opportunity until July 1. Then they stamped Vaux flat.

As for the German contribution to the reputation of the Marine Brigade, the Germans had seen a great deal of fighting, and they did not get excited about Belleau Woods. The mission of the German 4th Reserve Corps was to form a defensive flank for the line along the Marne, and to cover the left of a push westward toward the Ourcq. The valley of the Clignon Brook, which runs a few kilometers north of, and roughly parallel to, the Paris-Metz road, offered a suitable site for their main line, as well as a convenient covered area for the assembly of troops in the event of a decision to drive further down the Marne. This line had certain natural exits; the depression leading south from Bussiares, and the Bois de Belleau, and the point Hill 142. The Germans included these places in their outpost zone, when, in the first two days of June, they drove the French across the Clignon. The Bois de Belleau they organized and held in force. Then they sensed a stiffening in the enemy on their front, and presently identified the corpse of a 6th Marine, and on June 6, got a few prisoners from the 23rd Infantry and the Marine Brigade. Finding Americans on their front—American regulars—they considered it desirable to thrash, thoroughly, this new opponent; to assert a moral superiority at the outset of his entry upon the war. Bussiares—Torcy—Bouresches—the Bois de Belleau, even—they were not particularly important. But it was important to beat the Americans, and German division commanders so advised their troops. It followed that for a little space the attention of the world was centered on a few square kilometers of blood-soaked woodland, and it was the fortune of the Marine Brigade to answer the question: Will these Yankees fight? And it is recorded that they answered it.

Thereafter, the Marine Brigade did not emerge from the dispatches as a unit. The 2nd Division continued to have opportunities. It was one of the three divisions—the others were the American 1st Division and the Moroccan 1st Division—that attacked south of Soissons on July 18; and that day the war was lost to the Central Empires. It went to Gouraud in the Champagne, at the end of September, where the Germans held firm in the massif Notre Dame des Champs, and pierced that place in one of the great, clean-cut assaults of the war. It drove up from the Argonne to the Meuse in November with the Americans; the last night of the war the Marine Brigade got men perilously across the Meuse and was attacking when the Armistice fell. It marched to Germany and it came home in August of the next year, and disbanded. It so fell out that all its opportunities were conspicuous. It came upon the front at critical times. Great events hinged upon its attacks. Much of that was chance; the A.E.F. had several divisions that would have done well anywhere. But there was nothing of luck—there was cold, hard discipline, and much war-wisdom, learned under the guns, and sheer, clean skill, in the fighting which made these opportunities good.

These things came at a price. Statistics are not interesting; the butcher's bill of the American 2nd Division will compare cruelly and honorably, for the five months it was engaged, with that of any division in any Army in the war. The casualties of the Marine Brigade were nearer two hundred than one hundred per cent. Such things carry little meaning except to men who can remember the dreadful wheat field to the west of Belleau Woods, and shrapnel-flailed slopes between Blanc Mont and St. Ettienne, and the line of dead engineers on the path between the heights of the Meuse near Pouilly and the place where the bridge was, that last night of the war.

For the rest, there is transmitted a certain old blood-stained glory, peculiarly of the marines and of the United States naval service. That was the Marine Brigade.

5 "First Contact with the Enemy"

Richard B. Frank

Naval History (April 2010): 28–35

THE EPIC GUADALCANAL CAMPAIGN lasted six months, from 7 August 1942 to 9 February 1943. It featured seven major naval battles, a score or more large-scale battles ashore, the almost daily cut and thrust of aerial clashes, and dozens of encounters between ships and planes. The long struggle remains without peer in military history for heavy, sustained combat in all three dimensions—land, sea, and air. Japan and the United States battled at even odds, resulting in a see-saw campaign with first one antagonist and then the other gaining the upper hand.

With no other major U.S. effort on any other front competing for attention, Guadalcanal riveted the American public. The country's oscillating fortunes sent its senior leaders soaring into unwarranted optimism at the opening stages only to plummet into despair as the specter of a catastrophic American defeat rose before them. Guadalcanal carried strategic and psychological implications far beyond the immediate issue of who would prevail on the obscure island.

Admiral Ernest J. King, the Commander-in-Chief of the U.S. Fleet, willed the campaign into existence. He aimed to exploit the great June 1942 victory at Midway and block further Japanese advances down through the South Pacific threatening the lines of communication to Australia and New Zealand. King foresaw earlier than others that the United States could generate the resources to support an offensive in the Pacific even within the context of a fundamental commitment to the Allies' "Germany first" strategy. That offensive would deny Japan a respite in which to fortify her newly won Pacific frontier.

Radio intelligence warned of Japanese intentions to build an airbase on Guadalcanal, one of the southern Solomon Islands near the equator, northeast of Australia. Jungle-covered Guadalcanal is 90 miles long, but it featured a grassy northern coastal plain suitable for an airfield. King convinced General George C. Marshall, the Chief of Staff of the U.S. Army, to authorize on 2 July 1942 a three-step campaign plan ultimately aimed at seizing Rabaul, the main Japanese bastion in the South Pacific. The first step was the seizure of Guadalcanal—Operation Watchtower.

King catapulted the effort at astonishing speed. Sea, land, and air forces hastily assembled from the West Coast, Hawaii, Australia, and New Zealand. The landing force was the 1st Marine Division under Major General Alexander Archer Vandegrift. The division's ranks contained few men of long service but overflowed with post–Pearl Harbor enlistees, overwhelmingly teenagers. King had assured the Marines that Vandegrift's neophyte division would have six months for desperately needed training before commitment to combat. Instead, Vandegrift found himself preparing for the first American offensive of the war within three weeks of arrival in New Zealand. There was no time for proper intelligence-gathering, planning was chaotic, and a much-needed landing rehearsal in the Fiji Islands proved nearly useless because of unanticipated reefs. One officer would ruefully comment that experienced logistical planners later in the war would have pronounced the Guadalcanal operation as impossible.

Despite all the handicaps, fortune initially showered favor on the enterprise. Cloud cover masked the task forces' approach from Japanese search planes. Consequently, the 1st Marine Division achieved complete strategic and tactical surprise when it landed on Guadalcanal and the nearby islands of Tulagi and Gavutu-Tanambogo on 7 August 1942. After stiff fights, Tulagi and Gavutu-Tanambogo were secured on 8 August. That same day the main Marine contingent on Guadalcanal occupied the unfinished airfield after very light enemy resistance. Most of the island's Japanese garrison were Korean laborers who fled the coastal plain, near Lunga Point, after the preliminary naval bombardment.

Then, however, the tide of fortune dramatically reversed. Vice Admiral Gunichi Mikawa, commander of the Japanese 8th Fleet at Rabaul, daringly led a pick-up task force of cruisers and a destroyer down to the waters off Savo Island, just off the northwestern coast of Guadalcanal. Early on 9 August, Mikawa inflicted the worst defeat at sea the U.S. Navy ever sustained, sinking three American and one Australian cruiser while sustaining trifling damage in return. The calamity plus the withdrawal of the covering carrier task force compelled Rear Admiral Richmond Kelly Turner, the amphibious force commander, to pull back his transports and their escorts that same afternoon.

Thus began one of the greatest chapters in the illustrious history of the U.S. Marine Corps. Vandegrift's now-isolated Marines formed a position along the coast with short inland extensions around Lunga Point. Within that enclave rested the airfield site they soon completed and named Henderson Field after a Marine flier killed at Midway. Facing a dreadful shortage of equipment and supplies, Vandegrift immediately placed the garrison on a two-meal-a-day schedule. Unchallenged Japanese aviators and sailors began a program of day and night bombing and bombardment.

Certain that the United States could not mount a major Pacific offensive before 1943, top Japanese officers easily convinced themselves that the American adventure was limited, perhaps only a raid. Accordingly, they first dispatched a reinforced battalion task force under Colonel Kiyoano Ichiki to retake the airfield. While Japanese destroyers transported Ichiki and his men to a location east of the American position, the first U.S. planes reached the island on 20 August. These were two Marine squadrons, one of fighters and one of dive bombers. Their appearance tremendously boosted Marine morale for they tangibly signified intent to support the garrison. More important, the planes, and the ultimately scores more to follow, provided the means to strike back against Japanese air supremacy.

Ignoring a vulnerable open inland flank, Ichiki launched his command into a frantic frontal charge during the night of 20–21 August. The attack fell at the mouth of a feature known as the Tenaru River to the defenders, who comprised mainly elements of the 2d Battalion, 1st Marines (including Private Robert Leckie). The tidal watercourse with a conspicuous sandbar was actually Alligator Creek. In accordance with the traditions and doctrine of the Imperial Japanese Army, Ichiki mainly relied on swords, bayonets, and raw courage rather than firepower to break through the Marine position. The Japanese believed that American morale would collapse once a penetration was achieved. The tactics had worked all too well so far against the Allies. But the green Marines not only stood firm, the next day they trapped and nearly annihilated Ichiki's command.

The Battle of the Tenaru was arguably the most fateful small battle of the Pacific war. In the aftermath of the action, Marines and Navy corpsmen attempted to capture and treat the surviving wounded Japanese. The stunned Americans, from Vandegrift on down, discovered that the Japanese not only attempted to kill themselves rather than accept surrender but also sought to kill their would-be Good Samaritans. From that moment the Marines learned the Japanese not only were not taking prisoners (as an earlier patrol action had warned), but that they would not surrender. The lesson resonated throughout the American armed forces and set the savage code for the whole Pacific war.

On 24 August, American and Japanese carriers clashed in the Battle of the Eastern Solomons. Although the fleet carrier USS *Enterprise* (CV-6) was damaged, the Americans under Vice Admiral Frank Jack Fletcher sank the light carrier *Ryujo* and got much the better of the exchange in aircraft and particularly aircrews. The action also defeated a Japanese reinforcement attempt.

With these battles in late August, the campaign took on a novel cast: a change of sea control every 12 hours, creating a mutual siege. By day, American planes on Guadalcanal countered repeated Japanese bombing raids, protected a trickle of supply ships that kept the Marines barely supplied and fed, and denied the enemy the chance to use slow cargo ships to reinforce its forces on Guadalcanal. By night, the Imperial Japanese Navy ruled the waters off Guadalcanal. Swift destroyers and occasionally cruisers the Americans dubbed the "Tokyo Express" sprinted down the "Slot" (New Georgia Sound) to deliver men and supplies to Guadalcanal and customarily to bombard the American positions. But the Japanese did not linger till daylight lest they fall prey to U.S. airpower that gradually included Navy, Marine, and Army Air Forces squadrons. This hodgepodge of air units became the "Cactus Air Force" (Cactus was the code name for Guadalcanal) and marked the first truly joint service operations in American military history.

Still underestimating the number of Americans ashore, the Japanese renewed their effort to recapture Guadalcanal's airfield in September with Major General Kiyotaki Kawaguchi's 35th Brigade. Kawaguchi proved the most astute Japanese soldier to fight on Guadalcanal. He cast a plan around a deep inland flanking march he calculated would permit him to launch an attack on the undefended southern perimeter of the American position and capture the vital airfield. When he devised his plan, it offered excellent prospects. Based on a prescient analysis of Kawaguchi's intentions from patrol encounters, Vandegrift deployed the 1st Marine Raider Battalion under Lieutenant Colonel Merritt A. Edson, reinforced by the depleted 1st Marine Parachute Battalion, on a ridge offering an obvious avenue of approach from the south.

On two successive nights between 12 and 14 September, Kawaguchi struck. On the second night, he came within a hair's breadth of victory. But inspired by Edson and bolstered by devastating artillery fire, the Marines barely held what became known as Edson's Ridge. Having sustained devastating casualties, Kawaguchi led his starving survivors on a terrible forced march to the west, where the Japanese now intended to mount their main effort.

The Japanese, having failed with a battalion in August and a brigade in September, extended their pattern of piecemeal commitment by planning an October attack by a division. But this time Emperor Hirohito's army and navy commanders planned a coordinated effort. The Japanese Navy's airmen in the Solomons mounted repeated raids to quell American airpower on Guadalcanal, as nightly runs deposited soldiers of the 2nd "Sendai" Division on Guadalcanal. On the night of 11–12 October, an American cruiser-destroyer task force won a victory over a similar Japanese force at the Battle of Cape Esperance. But about 48 hours later, after the U.S. Army's 164th Infantry Regiment reached Guadalcanal, two Japanese battleships pummeled Henderson Field with nearly 1,000 huge shells. It was the most intense single bombardment American forces have ever faced.

Although the Marines endured scores of other nights on the receiving end of imperial navy gunfire, they ever after referred to this one as "The Bombardment." It reduced American airpower on Guadalcanal to near impotence. The Japanese were able to anchor a five-ship convoy off the island in broad daylight and unload the vessels before the gaze of the American defenders.

The Bombardment, followed by the arrival of the convoy, unnerved top civilian and uniformed officials in Washington. Secretary of the Navy Frank Knox could not give reporters a definitive assurance that Guadalcanal would be held. Facing the prospect of defeat, Washington leaders authorized the release of more extensive and far darker information about the situation. *The New York Times* published an editorial that amounted to a eulogy for the Americans on the island: "Guadalcanal: the name will not die out of the memories of this generation. It will endure with honor."

But Admiral Chester Nimitz, the Pacific Fleet's Commander-in-Chief, met the crisis by replacing failing Vice Admiral Robert L. Ghormley as South Pacific commander with the aggressive Vice Admiral William F. Halsey Jr. Fortunately, the one place where dark doubts gained no hold was the place where it counted the most: Guadalcanal. By this point, Vandegrift had installed a full perimeter around the airfield, but he and his staff projected that the most likely Japanese move was a thrust near the coast across the Matanikau River, west of the main position. From there the Japanese could mass artillery to neutralize the now-multiple American airfields. Their loss would result in forfeiting the ability to resupply U.S. forces on the island. American defeat on Guadalcanal then would be inevitable.

The senior Japanese officer then on Guadalcanal, 17th Army commander Lieutenant General Harukichi Hyakutake, and his staff perceived things differently. They believed an attack near the coast would turn into a firepower match they could not win because of the American stranglehold on their logistics. Accordingly, Hyakutake authorized part of his forces to engage American attention along the Matanikau while the Sendai Division, one of the most illustrious in the Imperial Japanese Army, conducted a stealthy march through the jungle south of the American perimeter and then staged a surprise attack on a thinly defended sector.

The Sendai soldiers, however, found themselves on a nightmare trek that delayed and disorganized them. A miscommunication about a postponement of the main attack led to a premature feinting thrust along the Matanikau that was crushed by Marine infantry and artillery. Nevertheless, the Japanese diversion worked to the extent that the Marine command was shifting units to meet it until dusk fell on 24 October. South of the airfields, Lieutenant Colonel Lewis "Chesty" Puller's 1st Battalion, 7th Marines held a sector that was originally prepared for a regiment. Although in theory the Sendai Division had nine infantry battalions to send against Puller's one, the disorganized Japanese only managed to send parts of three battalions forward. Puller's men, reinforced by the Army's 2nd Battalion, 164th Infantry just managed to contain the attack. During the night, Sergeant John Basilone earned the Medal of Honor for the pivotal role his machine-gun section played in halting the Japanese. The attackers tried again the next night, but Puller's Marines, reinforced with Army troops, again held.

No sooner was the Battle of Henderson Field over than two American carriers took on four Japanese counterparts at the Battle of the Santa Cruz Islands. Tactically, the Americans lost. The USS *Hornet* (CV-8) and a destroyer were sunk. While no Japanese ships went down, two carriers were damaged and imperial navy air groups sustained more losses than at Midway. Both sides now had only one operational carrier.

After three failures on land, the Japanese paused to ponder whether to quit Guadalcanal. Convinced that they had inflicted far more damage on the American fleet in the carrier battle, and drawn on by monitored American media accounts of the perilous situation on Guadalcanal, the Japanese chose to try again. They scaled up the October effort to include more air attacks, a battleship bombardment, and a large, 11-ship convoy to not only land reinforcements but also to make good the accumulated supply deficit.

Soon after taking command in the South Pacific, Halsey had said to Vandegrift, "I promise you everything I've got." Now the admiral made good on that pledge. As the opposing fleets headed into battle with the outcome of the campaign at stake, tension at the White House reached a level only surpassed during the war on the eve of the D-Day invasion of Europe. In the early hours of 13 November, a sacrificial fight by an outgunned American cruiser-destroyer task force thwarted the battleship bombardment. Two American admirals, Daniel Callaghan and Norman Scott, were killed. The next day, American planes from Guadalcanal and the *Enterprise* pummeled the Japanese convoy, leaving just four cargo ships still on course for Guadalcanal as darkness fell. That night off Savo Island, Rear Admiral Willis A. Lee's task force composed of the battleships *Washington* (BB-56) and *South Dakota* (BB-57) and four destroyers met a Japanese force that included a battleship, four cruisers, and nine destroyers. Although three of the four American destroyers were sunk and the *South Dakota* was knocked out of the action, Lee coolly won the battle. As one Japanese officer said, it was "the fork in the road."

In December Tokyo first contemplated yet another offensive, but by the end of the month, the Emperor himself sanctioned the decision to withdraw. Rendered ineffective because of malaria and exhaustion as much as combat losses, the 1st Marine Division had begun leaving the island in early December. The remaining American forces, the 2nd Marine Division and the Army Americal and 25th Infantry divisions, launched a cautious advance to clear the island in January. Nothing so became the Japanese conduct of the campaign as their departure. They cleverly concealed their plans. Sacrificial action by some soldiers permitted 10,643 emaciated, exhausted, and barely mobile survivors of the 17th Army to be whisked away by Japanese destroyers over three nights in February.

Guadalcanal cost the U.S. Navy 25 warships and the Imperial Japanese Navy 24. The air campaign claimed 683 Japanese and 615 American aircraft. A total of 7,100 Americans died (1,769 Soldiers and Marines, 420 Airmen of all services, and 4,911 Sailors). The toll for Japan reached 29,883, including 25,600 ground forces, about 1,200 airmen, and 3,083 sailors.

It's hard to overstate the strategic significance of Guadalcanal. The Battle of Midway checked the Japanese offensive in the Central Pacific ultimately aimed at seizing the Hawaiian Islands and reaching a negotiated peace. The destruction of the four best Japanese fleet carriers constituted the first irreversible defeat suffered by the Axis powers in the war. After Midway, however, the Japanese remained on the offensive in the

South Pacific, and therefore Guadalcanal represented the true change in strategic posture. It inflicted devastating losses from which the Japanese Navy's air arm never recovered. But still more was in balance.

In the spring of 1942, the Axis powers held in their grasp the possibility of a Japanese naval advance across the Indian Ocean meeting a German land thrust down through the Middle East. This combination would sever the Western Allies' last link with China, likely driving it from the war, and would strike a devastating blow to British participation in the war by collapsing its positions in India and the Middle East. The twin drives would further block the principal route for Lend-Lease war material supplies to the Soviet Union. By defeating the Japanese at Midway and keeping them tied down at Guadalcanal, the United States forestalled this last realistic hope for an Axis victory in the war.

Yet another dimension to Guadalcanal elevates it over Midway. The greatest American novelist of World War II, James Jones, set *The Thin Red Line*, his autobiographical work of Pacific combat, on Guadalcanal because, as he explained, "what Guadalcanal meant to my generation was a very special thing." Jones was referring to the fundamental and hugely visceral question of whether his generation could meet and defeat the soldiers of the Axis powers who exalted themselves as the master warrior races. Americans regarded Guadalcanal at the first valid response to that question, and the Marines and Soldiers who fought on Guadalcanal demonstrated to their contemporaries and the American public that the answer was yes.

6 "The Pacific War's Biggest Battle"

Richard B. Frank

Naval History (April 2010): 56–61

NOTE: *Where the author mentions* The Pacific, *he is referring to the ten-part HBO television mini-series by that title.*

THE CAPTURE OF OKINAWA (Operation Iceberg) originally was all about the role of airpower in the final phase of the Pacific war. Unlike Iwo Jima, where Marines landed on 19 February 1945, Okinawa offered space to base thousands of strategic bombers and tactical aircraft. It sat just 340 miles from Kyushu, Japan's southernmost Home Island. From Okinawa, U.S. and British strategic bombers could tremendously increase the impact of their bombardment campaign. Tactical aircraft could supplement the overall aerial campaign, clamp down a still-tighter blockade, and also afford direct support for the first stage of the planned two-phase invasion of Japan.

The importance of Okinawa did not escape the Japanese. But their defense plans for the island did not aim for victory. Japan's senior officers sought to employ the struggle on Okinawa to purchase extra time to gird the Home Islands for invasion and to advance their national strategy of exhaustion of the adversaries by attrition. On Okinawa Lieutenant

General Mitsuru Ushijima's 32nd Army would conduct one of the few campaigns in the last three years of the war marked by astute Japanese generalship. Ushijima's 100,000 men—about 75,000 Japanese and the rest Okinawans—included three main combat formations: the 24th Division, 62nd Division, and 44th Independent Mixed Brigade (IMB).

Very fortunately for the Americans, Tokyo had transferred the 9th Division, the best on the island, to Formosa, which Imperial Japanese Army leaders mistakenly concluded was the more likely target. Although the move initially depressed morale in the 32nd Army, its clever operations officer, Colonel Hiromichi Yohara, devised an operational plan that infused the army with energetic purpose. He labeled his scheme "sleeping tactics" and promulgated the plan to the army in a pamphlet titled "The Road to Certain Victory."

The army would abandon the northern three-quarters of Okinawa, including, to the consternation of Tokyo, existing airfield sites. On a trio of ridges forming natural ramparts in the southern quarter of the island, the army frantically prepared intricate defensive belts. On Okinawa the Japanese also fielded their most numerous and well-directed artillery component of the Pacific campaigns. The island had served as an artillery training facility, and consequently, the precise terrain survey permitted deadly accurate fires.

Under Yohara's plan, the army would eschew the sort of heroic but self-defeating banzai counterattacks that marked most prior campaigns to preserve strength as long as possible in order to inflict the maximum blood cost on the invaders from within its fortifications. Although Ushijima accepted that annihilation of his army and his death constituted the probable outcome of the battle, he and his staff kindled hopes that their stubborn defense would allow a massive onslaught of kamikaze attacks that would inflict such attrition on the invasion fleet that the Americans would give up.

For both sides, the aspect of Okinawa that boded hugely for the expected invasion of Japan was the presence of nearly half a million civilians. The island's natives actually are ethnically distinct from mainland Japanese, and the Okinawans chafed under what they perceived as deeply ingrained discrimination. The friction remains to this day, and not least of the reasons is that many Okinawans believe the 32nd Army actively encouraged civilians on the island to follow the same policy of suicide before surrender as governed Japan's armed forces. There is little doubt, however, that the 32nd Army would have been just as ruthless if the inhabitants had been Japanese.

The U.S. Tenth Army under Lieutenant General Simon Bolivar Buckner drew the task of taking Okinawa. The son of a Confederate general, Buckner's prior role had been in the Aleutians backwater; Okinawa was his first—and only—test as an army commander. Buckner's assault echelon alone required 183,000 troops. After the landing, another 80,000 men would develop a massive array of airfields on Okinawa, requiring no fewer than 25 miles of runways plus taxiways and hardstands. From Europe, Major General James Doolittle's Eighth Air Force (re-equipped with B-29s) would stage to Okinawa, as would a British strategic bombing force of Lancaster bombers, half used as refueling aircraft. Thousands of tactical aircraft under Lieutenant General George Kenny's Far East Air Force would also migrate up to the island. Okinawa would furthermore become a major fleet base.

Two corps constituted the main combat components of the Tenth Army. The 1st, 2nd, and 6th Marine divisions formed Major General Roy Geiger's III Amphibious Corps. The Army's XXIV Corps under Major General John Hodge comprised the 7th, 77th, and 96th Infantry divisions. The Army 27th Infantry Division was Buckner's reserve. A massive 1,418-ship invasion fleet under Admiral Raymond Spruance incorporated both amphibious shipping under Vice Admiral Richmond Kelly Turner, who started the war at Guadalcanal, and vast support forces, including 17 U.S. and 5 British fleet carriers and some 20 battleships. In terms of combat naval might, Spruance's command represented far more power than the Normandy invasion fleet.

The naval forces, however, gained a sobering preview of what Okinawa would cost. On 19 March 1945 during preliminary carrier strikes on Kyushu, two Japanese bombs hit the fleet carrier USS *Franklin* (CV-13). Huge fires and explosions killed at least 798 crewmen. The losses were an omen that victory would come at an unexpectedly heavy cost.

To the amazement of all hands, virtually no opposition confronted the main American landing on 1 April 1945—April Fool's Day. The III Amphibious Corps crossed Okinawa and then wheeled to clear the northern two-thirds of the island. The XXIV Corps pivoted south. During these early days, ground fighting was so light that Admiral Turner jocularly signaled Admiral Nimitz: "I may be crazy but it looks like the Japs have quit the war, at least in this section." Nimitz replied tersely, "Delete all after crazy."

By 7 April, the 7th and 96th Infantry divisions confronted the first of the major defense lines, which were centered on ancient Shuri Castle, location of the 32nd Army headquarters. Modest U.S. Army advances in exchange for mounting casualties prompted Buckner to commit the 27th Infantry Division on 10 April and the 77th Infantry Division on the 30th. When these too proved insufficient to renew the advance and the III Amphibious Corps completed its sweep of northern Okinawa, Marine infantry units headed south. The III Amphibious Corps took over the right (west) of the Tenth Army line, with the 6th Marine Division on the west coast and the 1st Marine Division on the corps' left, adjacent to the Army's XXIV Corps. (After staging an amphibious feint off southern Okinawa on 1 April, the 2d Marine Division had returned to Saipan to stand in reserve. Only its 8th Marine Regiment, reinforced with an artillery battalion and amphibian tractor battalion, would participate in the last days of the campaign, while attached to the 1st Marine Division. The failure to employ this division en masse on Okinawa remains one of the campaign's controversies.)

The Japanese had responded to the landing by launching Ten Go, a series of ten mass suicide attacks between April and June that ultimately numbered 1,900 kamikaze sorties. These strikes killed at least 3,389 Americans. Although the prime weapon was the suicide plane, in the first of these, on 6–7 April, the superbattleship *Yamato* and five of her nine consorts were sunk by U.S. carrier planes before they reached Okinawa. During the campaign, at least 30 American ships were sunk and 368 ships and craft damaged, overwhelmingly by kamikazes.

Essentially this is the point where *The Pacific* picks up the Battle of Okinawa, with the arrival of the 1st Marine Division in southern Okinawa on 1 May. There, the division would battle at the infamous Wana Draw–Dakeshi area and then Shuri Castle. But *The Pacific*, as usual, is not a story of maneuvers by battalions or larger units. It's Okinawa as seen by the average Marine or Soldier in all its unrelieved physical misery and graphic horror.

The exceptionally well-seasoned and well-led 1st Marine Division entered the battle with a third of its men veterans of two campaigns, a second third veterans of one campaign, and the final third with no combat experience. The markedly higher casualties the American forces had incurred in Europe and the Pacific since a much-increased level of combat starting in June 1944 created a serious problem of manpower mobilization. It prompted the infusion, to maintain strength, of a relatively modest stream of draftees into the heretofore all-volunteer Marine Corps. Since the overwhelming majority of Marines were enlistees, the draftees typically experienced a great deal of good-natured back-and-forth before they were accepted.

Sporadic showers and steady drizzle meanwhile dumped more than four inches of rain in early May, resulting in muddy, chilly personal misery and creating a serious impediment to American combined-arms tactics. But on 21 May the rains became a deluge that lasted nine days and dumped 11 inches of rain. Valleys became swamps, roads became morasses impassable in places even to tracked vehicles, and every sloping surface proved challenging to even simple foot traffic. Resupply, evacuation, and reinforcement of the front line broke down. Hand-carrying supplies forward and the wounded back drained already-low reservoirs of stamina. (In one location, it took 12 men to get a single stretcher through a ravine and fast-flowing stream.) Marines and Soldiers remained continuously wet and caked with mud. Eating became sporadic, sound sleep impossible. Even primitive sanitation broke down, and men sat surrounded by fly-clouded decomposing bodies and human filth.

Cleverly placed, mutually supporting Japanese positions subjected advances to devastating surprise fires from the flanks or even the rear. Hills were won and lost multiple times. By night the usual Japanese infiltration tactics kept all hands on edge. Each newly won position had to be defended against inevitable counterattacks ending often in grenade battles at close range and hand-to-hand fighting. The Japanese funneled replacements from support units into their principal combat formations, which masked for some time the extremely high rate of attrition they too suffered. And always, the Americans experienced more deadly artillery fire than ever before in the Pacific.

No fewer than 11,147 replacements were sent to fill depleted Marine ranks in the III Amphibious Corps. The huge demands for replacements on Iwo Jima and then Okinawa seriously shortened training programs, and the new arrivals proved far more prone to become casualties than the men they replaced. Officer casualties were so high that Eugene Sledge found he could not even keep track of all the officers who served with his outfit—K Company, 3d Battalion, 5th Marines.

On top of all the misery, the battle surged over Okinawan civilians. The Japanese had told them the Americans would rape their women and then slaughter them all. Deadly fires by weapons of all calibers, naval gunfire, and air bombardment killed Okinawans by the thousands. Distinguishing whether civilians were being used as shields by attacking Japanese units presented an insoluble and sickening moral dilemma. Some compassionate Japanese soldiers sought to protect and save the noncombatants. Others, however, sought to kill them to prevent their falling into American hands. Repeatedly, both the Okinawan civilians and the Japanese combatants sought shelter together in caves and tunnels, making it impossible to battle the warriors without inflicting loss on the noncombatants.

The long, costly campaign stirred much highly vocal criticism in America, particularly after Germany surrendered on 8 May and Okinawa represented the only major ongoing battle. One of the most pointed issues then and thereafter was whether General Buckner should have attempted to break the deadlock at the Shuri front by landing a division behind Japanese lines. At various times that proposition was advanced to Buckner not only by Marine officers (who urged use of the 2d Marine Division) but also by Army officers. After subjecting the proposal to serious consideration for three to five days before 22 April, Buckner rejected it primarily for two reasons. First, his logistical officer informed him he could support such an endeavor with food but not ammunition (later operations in this area confirmed that running supplies over the available beaches was a challenge). Second, until 4 May the Japanese kept the 24th Division or the 44th IMB in position precisely to confront such a landing.

Buckner also fielded additional reasons to reject the plan. Heavy losses in the 7th, 27th, and 96th Infantry divisions had so lowered their combat efficiency that they had to be successively rotated off the front lines. Further, because the 77th Infantry Division had to leave behind garrison forces on the Kerama Islands and Ie Shima, it would not be deployed at full strength. Buckner said that if the 77th landed, it would have to be relieved within 48 hours, a very dubious possibility. He called the plan "another Anzio, but worse." But by 4 May, the defenders had to commit both the 24th Division and the 44th IMB to solidify the crumbling main Japanese line. It now appears that Buckner's decision was reasonable up to the 4th, but whether a landing between 5 and 21 May, when the Shuri position fell, was a missed opportunity will remain a lingering question.

After 82 days, Okinawa was declared secure on 21 June. American direct battle casualties totaled 12,520 killed and missing (including Buckner, killed by a Japanese antitank-gun round on 18 June) and 36,613 wounded. "Non-battle" casualties, including those who broke down mentally or became sick or injured, reached 33,096. Of the Japanese garrison of about 100,000, more than 92,000 died (including Ushijima, by his own hand on 22 June). About 7,401 defenders became prisoners of war, the highest rate for a Pacific campaign, but a significant portion of this number were impressed Okinawans. Even so, prisoners overwhelmingly were only taken after organized resistance ended on 21 June. The Okinawans have erected a monument on which are inscribed the names of all the combatants and noncombatants who died in the campaign. Those names total more than 252,000, thus indicating civilian deaths exceeded 147,000.

If total American losses then are placed at 82,229, the ratio of casualties is one American to less than 1.2 Japanese. With current American estimates of the strength of the Japanese armed forces at about five million (the actual number exceeded six million by August 1945) and bluntly expressed doubts by the Joint Chiefs of Staff that an organized capitulation of Japan's army and navy could be obtained, this ratio served as a dire warning of the potential human costs of ending the war.

Time magazine described the long Okinawa struggle as "one foot at a time against the sort of savage, rat-in-a-hole defense that only the Japanese can offer." Americans from President Harry S. Truman on down saw Okinawa as the Japanese intended—a preview of what an invasion of Japan would be like. As historian Ronald Spector remarked, the campaign paradoxically left the losers elated and the winners depressed. The Japanese saw the struggle as validation for their strategic aim of one final battle against the initial American invasion of the Home Islands. There, they would either defeat the attempt or inflict such casualties that the Americans would negotiate an end to the war to the taste of Japan's ultra-nationalistic and -militaristic leaders. The fact that the struggle for relatively small Okinawa had lasted 82 days, involved heavy American casualties, and previewed what fighting amid large Japanese populations would entail made U.S. officers and men tabbed for the invasion of the Home Islands believe their chances of survival were slim.

As one American staff officer observed, casualty figures from Okinawa left President Truman "perturbed." He spoke directly of his fears that an invasion of Japan would create "an Okinawa from one end of Japan to the other." Okinawa undoubtedly loomed very heavily in Truman's mind when the issue of using atomic bombs arose. In a way no prior work in any form has accomplished, *The Pacific* illuminates for generations to come just what the specter of "the invasion of Japan" meant to Americans of all stations in 1945.

7 "Fleet Marine Force Korea—Part I"

Lynn Montross

U.S. Naval Institute *Proceedings*
(August 1953): 829–43

KOREA HAS BEEN FOR CENTURIES the sore thumb of Asia, protruding as it does into the Yellow Sea and Sea of Japan at the focal point of the China-Japan-Russia triangle. Control of this strategic area is a first step toward domination of the Far East, and the forces of Communism could scarcely have chosen a more advantageous spot for a test of strength with the United Nations.

Nearly all the conditions favor an Asiatic military establishment over Western land and sea forces. The S-shaped peninsula is 525 miles in length—about the distance from New York to Columbus, Ohio—with a width ranging from 125 to 200 miles. A coastline of 6,000 miles offers more elements of hazard than hospitality—few adequate harbors on the east coast, and mud flats swept by 30-foot tides on the west coast. Tumbled foothills rise abruptly from the sea, and peaks of 8,000 feet form the vertebrae of the rocky spinal column.

The climate adds to the logistic problems of a Western army operating at a long distance from its homeland. Such fierce extremes as summer heat of 105° are recorded along with winter temperatures of 30° below zero. Destructive typhoons strike annually, and a monsoon season each summer turns dusty roads into quagmires.

Korea, in short, offers an Asiatic army a good many geographical advantages to offset the superiority in arms, equipment, and sea power of Western invaders. Not the least of these is a normal surplus of the two foods regarded as the staff of life in the Far East, since 40 per cent of the rice crop and 60 per cent of the fish catch have been exported in piping years of peace.

Possession of Korea for forty years was one of the foremost factors in the rise of the Japanese Empire to the stature of a world power. This lesson was not lost upon Moscow in 1945, when the United States and the Soviet Union began a joint occupation of Korea after the defeat of Japan in World War II. Soviet arms had contributed little to victory in the Pacific, but Moscow seized a political advantage with the aim of creating a Communist puppet state.

The first step in a policy of divide and conquer was taken when the Soviet military command made a permanent line of demarcation out of the 38th Parallel. The area north of this artificial boundary was organized into a zone of Soviet influence having little contact with a southern zone administered by U.S. troops. Soviet agents showed a cynical inconsistency by preaching a doctrine of unification while dividing Koreans into two inimical factions. The northern area was encouraged to raise an army of aggression, with the USSR supplying the arms and Red China the instructors. And in 1949 the two military zones became two unfriendly Korean nations, the North Korean Democratic People's Republic and the Republic of Korea, glaring at each other across the 38th Parallel after the withdrawal of Soviet and U.S. occupation forces.

Koreans call their country the "Land of the Morning Calm," but there was more poetry than truth in this name on June 25, 1950. Six well-trained North Korean (NK) divisions, armed with 200 Russian tanks, swept across the 38th Parallel in an unprovoked attack. The result was scarcely in doubt, since the Republic of Korea (ROK) could oppose the

aggressors only with an army of defense expanded from the constabu-
lary raised to put down Communist-inspired revolts. A few batteries of
105 mm. howitzers were the heaviest armament, and the establishment
lacked tanks or military aircraft.

United Nations (UN) intervention was prompt after the U.S. Government called a meeting of the Security Council at New York on June
25. Representatives of 53 nations condemned the NK aggression as a
breach of world peace and ordered military sanctions. President Truman
ordered the Seventh Fleet into action; and on the 30th it was assigned by
the Joint Chiefs of Staff (JCS) to the operational control of General of
the Army Douglas MacArthur, soon to be named supreme commander
of UN forces.

Only the day before, the U.S. Navy had fired the first American shots
of the war when a cruiser and two destroyers bombarded the NK invaders of the ROK coastal town of Samchok. General MacArthur was authorized to extend his operations into North Korea against military targets,
and on July 2 the 38th Parallel was crossed by Okinawa-based B-29s of
the Twentieth Air Force, which bombed the NK town of Yonpo.

On July 5 the U.S. Army got into the fight. Three reinforced companies of the 24th Infantry Division, flown from Japan, had their initial
brush with invaders who had captured Seoul and pushed southward.
These troops were sent on the recommendation of General MacArthur,
who visited the battlefront and reported to Washington that the retreating ROKs needed the aid of U.S. ground forces as well as naval and air
support.

The general also urged on July 2 that a Marine regimental combat
team (RCT) be sent immediately to Korea with its own air. The Chief of
Naval Operations (CNO) concurred that same day, and on the 7th the
1st Provisional Marine Brigade was activated at Camp Joseph H. Pendleton in southern California under the command of Brigadier General
Edward A. Craig. This organization consisted of the 5th Marines (reinf.)

and Marine Aircraft Group (MAG) 33—a total of 6,534 officers and men. The Brigade prepared for embarkation two days later, and on the 12th the first elements sailed from San Diego.

Five hurried days, of course, allowed little time for special training. The Brigade, however, was made up of men well grounded in fundamentals, since every post and station on the West Coast had been stripped to bring units up to strength. Even so, the three infantry battalions consisted of only two companies each, and third platoons had not been added until the last minute.

On July 10 the NK invaders had not yet suffered a reverse worth mentioning. Stateside observers were depressed by this result, though they did not suspect that the "police action" would become the fourth largest military effort of U.S. history before the end of the year. At a glance it appeared that UN forces held the trumps as Navy destroyers bombarded coastal towns while Navy planes of Task Force (TF) 77 and Air Force B-29s flew strikes on NK bridges, tunnels, roads, and marshaling yards. But Moscow had not erred in strategic calculations, and the NK army was actually a capable military instrument. The tough, well-led infantry divisions were at their best in camouflage, infiltration, and night operations. North Korean generalship was by no means contemptible, and supply problems were largely solved by living on an invaded country.

As the NK invaders drove southward, General MacArthur had not forgotten that most of his World War II victories in the Pacific were made possible by seaborne invasions. He visioned Korea as a sack in which the enemy was burrowing toward the bottom, and as early as July 4 he thought of pulling the drawstring by means of an amphibious operation in the middle of the peninsula.

Rear Admiral James H. Doyle and his Amphibious Group I staff were set to work on the preliminary plans. In the lack of a Marine division, the 1st Cavalry (infantry) Division was considered. But this unit was needed at the front, and on July 10 the Navy planners were ordered to other duties.

The concept had not been abandoned by General MacArthur, however, and it is significant that this same July 10 was the date of the first of his three requests for a Marine division. He had formed a high opinion of Marine amphibious techniques in World War II, and before the outbreak of Korean hostilities the Marine Corps sent its Training Group Able to instruct Army occupation troops. Not only were these officers available for planning, but Lieutenant General Lemuel C. Shepherd, Jr., commander of the Fleet Marine Force Pacific, had been ordered to Tokyo on July 4 to confer with General MacArthur.

Plans for a Korean amphibious operation were revived in earnest, therefore, with the assurance from Washington on the 25th that a Marine division would be sent to Korea. Unfortunately, the military situation had deteriorated so alarmingly at the end of the first month that it was a question whether the UN forces could retain a foothold. The recently organized Eighth U.S. Army, commanded by Lieutenant General Walton H. Walker, included the 24th and 25th Infantry Divisions and the 1st Cavalry Division. These early Army arrivals, consisting largely of occupation troops from Japan, shared with five battered, under-strength ROK divisions a struggle against material odds. Necessity imposed a strategy of trading space for time, and the UN forces sold ground dearly in delaying actions. But the invaders had taken the important communications center of Taejon and were driving toward Taegu. The left flank of the Eighth Army was in the air, and an end run took the enemy to Mokpu, near the southern tip of the peninsula.

There was little space left to barter for time, since the vital supply port of Pusan must be held at all costs. Reinforcements were so badly needed that General MacArthur ordered the 1st Provisional Marine Brigade to proceed directly to Korea instead of landing in Japan.

The Marines reached Pusan on August 2, the day after the debarkation of the 2d Infantry Division and Army 5th RCT. And on the 7th, the anniversary of the Guadalcanal landing of the 1st Marine Division in 1942, the Brigade was attached to the 25th Infantry Division to launch the first sustained UN counterattack along with Army infantry units. The objective was Chinju and the purpose was to stop the drive of the Korean Reds toward Masan.

Enemy advance units had infiltrated within 50 miles of Pusan, but this was to be the high-water mark of invasion. For the Marines made rapid progress, after a hard three-day preliminary fight, while the Army 5th RCT pushed ahead on a parallel route. General Craig was placed in operational control of Army as well as Marine forces during the critical period as MAG-33 fliers from the CVE carriers *Sicily* and *Badoeng Strait* flew close air support. Two NK regiments were riddled with casualties, and the objective was within sight when Army and Marine units were pulled back to cope with a new enemy drive on Taegu.

The Chinju operation was the first of a series of Eighth Army counter-attacks designed to disrupt the enemy's build-up of a supreme effort to smash through the Pusan Perimeter before losing his material superiority. A total of 13 NK divisions were massed for the attempt, including hastily raised new units of low quality. Until an amphibious assault could be mounted, it was up to the Eighth Army to hold the perimeter stretching in an irregular semicircle from Masan on the south coast through the Taegu area to Pohang on the east coast. The lack of enough UN strength to defend in force everywhere made it necessary to shift counterattack-ing units from one imperiled point to another. Thus the Marines found a role as the "firemen" of the Pusan Perimeter—a mobile reserve capable of putting out a tactical blaze before it became a strategic conflagration.

During this crisis General MacArthur had never given up his idea of an amphibious operation, and he had firmly decided upon Inchon as the objective. Early in August he requested that a Marine advance planning group be sent from California by air. The 23 officers and ten enlisted men reached Tokyo on the 22d and reported to Admiral Doyle and his Amphibious Group I. As further evidence of his unswerving purpose, the supreme commander set up a new corps for the operation. This was to be X Corps, commanded by Major General Edward M. Almond, with the 1st Marine Division as its major unit.

These preliminaries had been concluded before General MacArthur called a new planning conference at Tokyo on August 23. Admiral Forrest C. Sherman was present as well as Vice Admiral Charles T. Joy, Commander of the Navy, Far East, and Vice Admiral Arthur D. Struble. The general addressed them, reaffirming his conviction that surprise would prevail at Inchon, since 90 per cent of the NK forces were engaged in south Korea. He emphasized the advantages of taking the largest west coast seaport, then driving inland to seize Kimpo, chief airport of the peninsula, and Seoul, the former ROK capital that the enemy had made the hub of his communications. The capture of these objectives, he pointed out, would disrupt the enemy's supply system and place his army of invasion between the hammer of the amphibious assault and the anvil of the Eighth Army in south Korea.

The Navy and Marine officers of Admiral Doyle's group briefed General MacArthur on the situation at Inchon. The gist of their findings was that the proposed operation was difficult and hazardous but not impossible. Islands, shoals, and reefs limited the approach to the outer harbor, leaving only a single channel for large ships. Adverse currents would be encountered, and the inner harbor was a mud flat at low tide, navigable only by means of a narrow, dredged channel.

The maximum tidal range of 32 feet was one of the greatest in the world. At least 29 feet was needed for the LSTs, and this depth was assured only on September 15 and the two following days. The next opportunity would not come until the middle of October, with cold weather near at hand.

This meant, of course, that the prospects of a surprise were reduced, since the enemy could determine the date in advance. Another disturbing feature was the fact that two islands defended the inner harbor. They must first be neutralized before an attack could be mounted on the mainland, yet neither the morning nor evening high tide was long enough for both operations.

The beaches of the seaport, if such they could be called, consisted at high tide of mere strips of urban waterfront surmounted by a seawall. Scaling ladders would have to be used, since the wall was too high for ramps to be dropped by landing craft. And once past this barrier, the assault force faced the task of storming an Oriental city with a prewar population of 250,000. Altogether, the problems and perils of an Inchon landing made it unique in Navy and Marine experience. Even if the assault force took the seaport in spite of all, there remained the task of driving 20 miles inland to capture a city of 1,500,000 people which would have been forewarned in time to summon NK reinforcements from south Korea.

Navy and Marine planners, it is true, could count from the beginning on an overwhelming superiority in firepower, thanks to control of the sea and air. Even so, their greatest hope for success lay perhaps in an intangible—the experience and know-how gained from years of Navy and Marine research in the military science of amphibious warfare.

Although the date of the Pearl Harbor attack will never be forgotten, another December 7 is also memorable in U.S. military annals. For it was on this day in 1933 that the Fleet Marine Force came into being as a laboratory of amphibious techniques in time of peace and a force in readiness in time of war.

The times were not encouraging. Object lessons on the Western Front had led to over-emphasis of the defensive, and the Gallipoli catastrophe was accepted as proof that ship-to-shore attacks could not prevail against modern firepower. U.S. Navy and Marine officers were in the minority when they differed to the extent of trying to work out more effective amphibious techniques.

Enough progress was made during these pioneer years so that a directive in 1927 of the Joint Board of the Army and Navy (forerunner of JCS) gave the Marine Corps the mission of "special preparations in the conduct of landing operations."

These preparations were unceasing from the last month of 1933, when the Fleet Marine Force evolved, to the early months of World War II. In the lack of a comprehensive manual for landing operations, the Commandant ordered classes discontinued at the Marine Corps Schools in 1933 until a satisfactory hornbook could be written. This task was undertaken "with fear and trembling," as one Marine Officer put it, "while using the imagination that God gave to us."

Training exercises with the Navy continued year after year, and Fleet Marine Force training programs were set up on both coasts. Crude as some of the experiments may seem today, there are few periods of world military history to compare with them for creativeness. Not only the concepts of modern amphibious warfare but the very tools and tactical units had often to be created where none had existed before—such concepts as combat unit loading, such tools as the various landing craft, and such tactical units as the shore party battalion.

This achievement came in the nick of time. For the outbreak of World War II found the Fleet Marine Force in possession of new techniques which impressed a British historian, Major General J. F. C. Fuller, as being "in all probability . . . the most far-reaching tactical development of the war." Much remained to be learned the hard way in such early actions as Guadalcanal and Tarawa, but Navy and Marine teamwork improved with experience.

Nor were Saipan, Guam, Iwo Jima, and other Marine landings the only tests. For the Marine Corps trained four Army divisions in amphibious techniques, so that Fleet Marine Force doctrine helped to shape such Army operations as Oran, Casablanca, Sicily, Salerno, and Normandy.

Five years after the final victory in World War II, the planners of Inchon had the benefit of combat lessons learned from a fruitful Navy and Marine amphibious partnership. All of the Navy and Marine commanders at Inchon were seasoned veterans of that partnership. All of them had helped to hammer out amphibious assaults in the fiery forge of World War II, and now these admirals and generals were about to put into action a mighty intangible which might be called Fleet Marine Force Korea.

It was perhaps their most potent weapon.

They needed every resource, since only 23 days were left for Inchon planning—a fraction of the time usually devoted to a great amphibious operation. The Marine Corps was well represented. Colonel Edward H. Forney, chief of Marine Training Group Able, had been made deputy chief of staff for X Corps, responsible for all amphibious planning. Other officers were assigned as working members of the staff along with the Marine planners from California.

It is not customary for planning to go ahead full blast before there is assurance that the landing force will materialize, but this was another risk that had to be taken. Gone were the days when a Marine "gangplank expeditionary force" could be raised overnight from nearby posts and equipped with light armament. War had become a vastly more complex business; and on July 25 the 1st Marine Division was a mere skeleton organization. A wartime strength of about 22,000 men could never be reached without the "minute men of 1950"—the reserves called up late in July and early in August. Only a few weeks remained in which to assign the newcomers to units or use them to replace regulars drawn from posts and stations.

Heavy equipment for the division had been in mothballs at Barstow and other California depots since World War II. Five hundred civilians were employed for reconditioning as the reserves poured into Pendleton, and the goal of war strength was attained on August 15. The 1st Marines had been formed as a second infantry regiment, and third rifle companies organized for the 5th Marines of the Brigade. But the 7th Marines was not activated as the third infantry regiment until the 17th; and some of the troops, on duty with the Fleet, must sail from the Mediterranean direct to Japan.

It was a remarkable achievement for the main body of the 1st Marine Division, commanded by Major General Oliver P. Smith, to have embarked from California on August 18 and the 7th Marines on September 3.

The other major units of X Corps were to be the 7th Infantry Division, the 187th Airborne RCT, and a Korean Marine Corps regiment. On August 23, however, the final planning for Inchon started with only the probability that two infantry regiments of the 1st Marine Division would reach the target area in time for the target date.

Further risks had to be assumed by the planners when they approached the problems of the two islands, Wolmi-do and Sowolmi-do, defending the inner harbor. Connected to each other and the mainland by a concrete causeway, they must first be neutralized. Since one period of high tide did not allow time enough for both efforts, the planners decided to assault Wolmi-do and the smaller island on the morning of D-day and wait until late afternoon for the Inchon attack. The delay would present a warned enemy with the whole day for stiffening his Inchon defenses, which added to the task cut out for naval gunfire and interdictory air strikes.

Advance G-2 reports indicated a light resistance on Wolmi-do, but even a few shore guns could do a great deal of damage to landing craft. Despite the old Naval dictum that "a ship's a fool to fight a fort," the Inchon planners decided to send in destroyers at close range to unmask the Wolmi-do batteries by deliberately provoking their fire. It was recognized that the cans might run aground, and once again the Navy prepared to repel boarders, as in bygone days. No cutlasses were issued, but the crews would have automatic rifles and sidearms in case the enemy swarmed out across the mud flats.

After the D-day landing on Green Beach in Wolmi-do, dependence was to be placed in a final pounding by naval gunfire and air strikes to soften up the mainland for an assault set for 1730, the most favorable moment of high tide. Logistical demands made it necessary for the planners to assume another risk by deciding to beach LSTs with high priority supplies at H-plus-30, even though they would be sitting ducks for such enemy shore guns as had not yet been silenced.

Only 90 minutes of daylight would be left for the task of seizing Inchon. Neither the 7th Infantry Division nor the 187th Airborne RCT could arrive in time, which left the 1st and 5th Marines to carry the ball.

The planners decided to land the latter on a 1,000-foot strip designated as Red Beach, opposite the most thickly populated section of Inchon. The other regiment would hit Blue Beach, near the base of the peninsula, and swing to the rear of the city to cut off enemy escape and bar the way to reinforcements.

For a few days it was feared that even this small assault force might be prevented by the typhoon season from keeping its date with destiny. The 1st Marine Division (less the 5th and 7th Marines) landed at Kobe on August 31, and three days later a storm named JANE provided a boisterous welcome with winds of 110 miles per hour. Two ships were damaged and 24 hours lost at the task of unloading mixed-type cargo and combat-loading it into assault-type shipping. These hours were valuable, since the cargo ships were scheduled to sail for Inchon on September 10 and the troopships two days later.

The 5th Marines and other Brigade troops were not pulled out of the line until the night of September 6, after their second counterattack in the Naktong Bulge area near Taegu. On the 1st the enemy had mounted his long expected all-out offensive to break through the Pusan Perimeter. Again the Marines and Army units sent an NK advance into reverse, though the lack of third companies in the Brigade made it difficult to attack in the standard formation of "two up and one back"—two companies advancing abreast and a third in reserve.

After four days of battle the weary troops moved by motor and rail to Pusan, where third infantry companies and replacements had just landed. And on September 12, having reassumed their old designations in the 1st Marine Division, the Brigade units set sail for Inchon.

Again the planners had some anxious hours when a second typhoon, bearing the romantic name of KEZIA, threatened on September 9 to have the last word at Inchon. The carrier *Boxer*, nearing Japan from the U.S. with 96 planes on deck, actually did have to contend with 90-mile winds. But only the skirts of the hussy KEZIA brushed the armada bound for Inchon, and by the 13th the planners could put this anxiety out of mind.

They had no lack of other worries, for this was D-minus-2—the first day of the preliminary bombardments. Plan was about to meet the test of performance as Joint Task Force (JTF) 7 went into action.

Command of the operation as a whole passed from General Mac-Arthur, CINCFE, to Admiral Joy, COMNAVFE, acting through Admiral Struble, CJTF-7. Next in the chain came the commander of the attack force, TF-90, and the commander of the landing force, 1st Marine Division. Admiral Doyle, CTF-90, had the responsibility for the conduct of operations ashore until General Almond, CG X Corps, signified his readiness to assume that responsibility.

Both JTF-7 and X Corps were to have organic air support. JTF-7 depended on a Navy fast carrier task force, TF-77, for deep support and interdiction strikes. Close air support for the landing was the responsibility of two Marine squadrons on the two CVEs, *Sicily* and *Badoeng Strait*.

Tactical Air Command, X Corps, was a provisional 1st Marine Aircraft Wing organization under the control of General Almond and tactical direction of Brigadier General Thomas J. Cushman, USMC. The three carrier-based squadrons were to be based at Kimpo, after the securing of that field, along with command and ground echelons flown in from Japan.

At daybreak on D-minus-2 the ten warships of the Fire Support Group pulled the teeth of Wolmi-do. The U.S. cruisers *Rochester* and *Toledo* were accompanied by the British cruisers *Kenya* and *Jamaica* as an earnest of coming months when land or sea forces of a dozen other UN allies would join the fight against Communism. While these ships dropped off in support, the U.S. destroyers, *Gurke, Henderson, Swenson, Collett, De Haven*, and *Mansfield*, moved within 800 yards of the island as planes from the carriers of TF-77 made bombing runs.

Four mines were spotted that morning by the destroyers and detonated with 40 mm. fire. Eight more were destroyed on the return trip. The enemy, however, had taken little advantage of his opportunity to mine the harbor.

Marine planes from the jeep carriers had been blasting Wolmi-do for two days when the destroyers went in. They had to anchor and fire for half an hour before goading the shore guns into replying. Then five NK shells found the *Collett*, and the *Gurke* and *De Haven* also took hits. The total damage was slight, however, and the casualties were one officer killed and eight men wounded.

This was the cost of knocking out the island's guns. The four cruisers poured in 8-inch shells as enemy targets revealed themselves, and Navy planes worked them over with napalm. The next day, when the destroyers paid a second visit, only a few inaccurate shots came from Wolmi-do, which received another pounding.

On the overcast morning of D-day the humpbacked island heaved with explosions as General MacArthur looked on from the bridge of the *Mount McKinley* along with Admiral Joy and General Shepherd. Admiral Doyle's Attack Force was cutting loose with everything it had—naval gunfire, air strikes, and "ripples" of rockets fired by three LSMRs. Late G-2 reports indicated a weak resistance of about battalion strength, but there were ominous possibilities in an intercepted enemy dispatch sent on September 13 to the NK capital of Pyongyang. The appearance of ten UN warships had been correctly interpreted, and NK forces in the Inchon area were exhorted "to be ready for combat . . . so that they may throw back enemy forces when they attempt their landing operation."

The question on the morning of D-day was whether the enemy had any cards left up his sleeve. And the answer was soon supplied by the landing force, the 3d Battalion of the 5th Marines. At 0627 the first wave left the line of departure, and the LCVPs grated on Green Beach four minutes and 900 yards later. The second wave came on at 0635, followed within ten minutes by LSVs which disgorged tanks, bulldozers and flame throwers from their bow ramps. Little NK fire was received on the beach, and the assault troops met only a scattered resistance while sweeping to the high ground in the center of the island.

The statistics tell the story. Seventeen Marines were wounded as the price of capturing 136 NK defenders and killing an estimated 180. At 0701 the landing force ran up an American flag, and General MacArthur and his party left the bridge of the flagship for coffee below.

The value of Marine amphibious training was demonstrated during the next eight hours. There had been no time for 1st Marine Division rehearsals, no time even for training in most instances. But while an infantry squad secured Sowolmi-do, groups of amphibious specialists landed on the larger island before the receding tide left it surrounded by mud flats. The last of some 300 Russian landmines were destroyed and corduroy roads built so that supplies could be unloaded from LSTs. Then the dozers worked on artillery positions while the 1,000-foot causeway to the mainland was being repaired for the crossing of tanks. Marine shore party and engineer units, in short, lifted the battered face of Wolmi-do and transformed it into an advanced base for the assault on the mainland.

During the all-day interval between tides, Navy planes flew interdiction strikes within a 25-mile radius of Inchon to cut off NK reinforcements. As H-hour approached, the planes and rocket ships joined in the final 45-minute barrage poured in by the cruisers and destroyers giving direct support. The target area was hidden by smoke and flame as the landing craft churned the water of the inner harbor. Rain squalls added to an already low visibility, so that some confusion and intermingling of units resulted when the succeeding waves hit the beaches. Fleet Marine Force experience paid off, however, after veteran Marine company officers and NCOs took charge.

Enemy mortar and automatic weapons fire was scattered and poorly directed as the two battalions of the 5th Marines, commanded by Lieutenant Colonel Raymond L. Murray, scrambled over the seawall on Red Beach. Not enough scaling ladders had been provided, and naval gunfire had not succeeded in blasting enough holes in the masonry. But the Marines surmounted the barrier as best they could and re-formed for the drive on their objective line, about 1,000 yards inland, which included two commanding heights known as Cemetery and Observatory hills.

The critical moment approached as the six infantry companies plunged through the premature dusk into the narrow streets and alleys of a strange Oriental city. But if there had been some confusion on the beaches, even more resulted among defenders disorganized by the barrage. Marine company officers had been briefed as to routes, and speed was their best resource as they reached the first objective while the LSTs were still hitting the area with 3-inch and 20 mm. fire. The advance on Cemetery Hill had to be held up a few minutes, in fact, while the LSTs were requested to call off their dogs. By that time the Red Beach landing force had won a foothold, and the 1st Battalion slugged ahead through the dark streets to take Observatory Hill at 2000 and tie in with the 2d Battalion. Casualties had been moderate and patrols sent out 500 yards from the objective line met no resistance.

Another calculated risk of the Inchon planners was vindicated by the LSTs which wallowed toward Red Beach in the wake of the landing force. Their number was limited by the mathematical fact that a 1000-foot beach could hold only eight ships. For a few minutes these thin-skinned Navy workhorses appeared to be doing the infantry a favor by drawing fire. Enemy mortar rounds from Cemetery Hill began to register on hulls containing drums of gasoline and trucks loaded with napalm. But fortune as usual blessed the bold, and no serious damage resulted before the shore guns were silenced.

The flames of a burning brewery provided illumination for the task of unloading supplies totaling 800 tons of block cargo, 400 tons of ammunition, 240 tons of rations, 120 tons of water, and 40 tons of fuel. The bulldozers went ashore first to punch holes in the seawall for the tanks and trucks. Then the Marine engineers and shore party devoted the night to organizing supply dumps which would solve the logistical problem until the empty LSTs could be retracted on the morning tide to make room for more supply ships.

During the Blue Beach landings the leading waves of the 1st Marines, commanded by Colonel Lewis B. Puller, also had their troubles with delay, confusion, and intermingling of units. But enemy resistance was light in this sparsely settled factory district south of the city, and the assault troops pushed ahead through the darkness without much regard for flanks. After crossing a bottomland of rice paddies, they reached the high ground of their objective line within four hours and dug in for the night.

The attempt to beach LSTs in the area of the 1st Marines miscarried. These cargo ships grounded too far out from Blue Beach to be unloaded that night, so that the supplies had to wait until the morning tide. By that time more LSTs had neared Red Beach for unloading, without enemy interference, and the logistical problem was not far from solution when Marine engineers announced that Inchon harbor facilities could soon be made operative without major repairs.

Even more heartening was the fact that the landing which held so many potentialities of disaster had resulted in D-day losses of only 17 killed, 165 wounded, and two missing. No Marine casualty list is ever regarded as "light," but this was not an exorbitant price for seizing a third of Inchon.

At 0630 the next morning the attack was resumed. The two battalions of the 5th Marines moved out in column through the principal east-west streets, rejoined by the battalion which had crossed from Wolmi-do during the night. Two battalions of the 11th Marines followed over the causeway at dawn, but the assault troops had little need of artillery support. For the 5th Marines met only unorganized resistance, and the 1st Marines found the terrain more trouble than the enemy during a 7,000-yard advance to seal off the base of the Inchon peninsula. Mopping up pockets of bypassed resistance was left to the KMC troops as the two Marine regiments made contact at 1000 and combined for a drive to the eastern outskirts of the city.

The landing phase ended at 1730, just 24 hours after hitting the beaches, when General Smith set up his CP near the force beachhead line.

Marine casualties for the second day were four killed and 21 wounded. Enemy losses so far added up to nearly 300 prisoners and an estimated 1,350 killed and wounded.

Fleet Marine Force boldness tempered with precision had succeeded at Inchon in spite of the enemy's foreknowledge that a landing would be attempted. Several UN feints were made at points on both coasts, including a bombardment of Samchok by the USS *Missouri*, just arrived from the United States. But it does not appear that these diversions had much effect on the outcome. The enemy's failure to mine the harbor adequately and make the most of his Wolmi-do batteries were symptoms of a general neglect of strong defensive assets. For even 2,500 second-rate troops might have turned Inchon into another Tarawa if they had been better organized and directed.

Before passing judgment on Red Korean lapses, however, it might be recalled that veteran German and Japanese troops of World War II never once managed to inflict a defeat, let alone a disaster, on a major American amphibious landing. Thus it may be that the explanation of the crushing Red Korean defeat at Inchon goes back to that tactical laboratory of the 1930's—the Fleet Marine Force exercises carried out under the subtropical sun of Culebra by the U.S. Navy and Marine Corps.

After Inchon came the advance on Seoul as the two assault regiments jumped off at dawn on D-plus-2 from assembly areas east of the seaport. The importance of the final objective was enhanced by news that the Eighth Army had launched its combined offensive on September 16 against the main body of the NK army in southeast Korea.

The plan of maneuver called for the 5th Marines to seize Kimpo Airfield, cross the river Han, and close in on Seoul from the hills to the northwest. Meanwhile the 1st Marines was to take a parallel route to the south and fight its way into Yongdungpo, a large industrial suburb, before crossing the Han and moving on Seoul from the south. During this convergent advance each regiment would be responsible for division flank protection in its zone, relying upon naval gunfire, air strikes, and artillery fire for this purpose.

So successful had been the interdiction efforts of TF-77 planes that the enemy managed to make only a few piecemeal defensive efforts so far along the routes to Seoul. Six T-34 tanks were spotted just east of Inchon on D-plus-1 by Marine planes. But when the Corsairs pulled out of their screaming dives, two "caviar cans" had been destroyed and the other four crippled by bombs and napalm.

Despite this result, the enemy made another suicidal attempt the next morning to bar the way to Kimpo. The leading battalion of the 5th Marines discovered the approach of six T-34s, accompanied by about 200 NK infantry, in time to prepare an ambush. It was too late for the enemy column to pull out of the trap when hell broke loose. Marine tanks, rocket launchers, 75 mm. recoilless guns, and machine guns did not stop short of annihilation, and the battalion pounded ahead to occupy the airfield that night without a fight. Advance echelons of MAG-33 flew in from Japan the next day, and on September 20 the first strikes were being flown by land-based Marine planes.

Up to this time the landing force had managed without much need of close air support. But as the two regiments drove inland against stiffening resistance, more and more calls would be made for the gull-winged Corsairs.

Close air support is another technique developed in the laboratory of the Fleet Marine Force. The origins go back to an extensive experience of jungle and mountain warfare in Haiti and Nicaragua during the 1920's and early 1930's. Marine detachments were so often isolated that air-drop became a means of supply, and low-flying planes substituted for artillery preparation. Such improvisations suggested an answer to the need for integrated air support in a ship-to-shore attack, where the utmost effect may be achieved by knocking out opposition just ahead of the assault troops at dangerously close distances. Fleet Marine Force doctrine held that the safe solution lay in bridging the gap between air and ground forces; and Marine pilots and forward air controllers were given an intensive training in infantry tactics, including practice marches and maneuvers.

Close air support was the main reliance of the 1st Marines, advancing against stubborn opposition along the Inchon-Seoul highway. On September 19 alone, 24 sorties were flown by carrier-borne Corsairs to knock out mortar or machine gun positions pinning down the infantry. As a typical performance, the forward air controller summoned the four planes on station to work over a ridge near Sosa where enemy automatic weapons were holding up two Marine companies. After being oriented on the target, the Corsairs made their dummy runs. Then they roared in only a hundred yards ahead of their own infantry to score direct hits with napalm and 500-lb. bombs. Before the NK remnants could recover, Marine ground forces seized the ridge without a single casualty.

Tank and artillery as well as close air support helped the 1st Marines to reach the outskirts of Yongdungpo on the 19th. A terrific two-day fight followed before the enemy could be evicted, and meanwhile the 5th Marines battled its way across the Han. A reconnaissance by swimmers on the night of the 19th had revealed that the enemy held the right bank in about battalion strength. At dawn the 3d Battalion crossed in LVTs, following an artillery preparation. Two companies swung around in a surprise maneuver to take Hill 125 from the rear as the third company drove 1,500 yards inland and seized the high ground dominating the Seoul road. Then the 2d Battalion passed through and advanced astride the road while the 1st Battalion crossed in reserve.

The next day saw the end of the amphibious phase when responsibility for operations ashore passed to CG X Corps after General Almond notified Admiral Doyle, CTF-90, of his readiness. The attack force was dissolved accordingly, and Admiral Doyle was designated Commander Naval Support Force, operating under COMNAVFE.

This date, September 21, found the 7th Marines, commanded by Colonel Homer L. Litzenberg, disembarking at Inchon a few days after the landings of the 187th Airborne RCT and 7th Infantry Division. As these units moved into assigned areas, the Marines were able for the first time to advance on a division front, with the 1st Regiment on the right, the 5th in the center, and the 7th on the left to the north of Seoul. The 187th RCT had the mission of protecting the Corps left flank while 7th Infantry Division elements covered the right and advanced on Seoul from the southeast.

As the operation entered its second week, the Marines had their hardest fighting and heaviest losses. At first the brunt fell upon the 5th Marines, reinforced by two KMC battalions, in the hills northwest of Seoul. The Marines went up against one hill after another that had been transformed into a little fortress bristling with mortar and machine gun positions. Nearly 1,750 NK dead were counted on one of these positions alone, and at the finish the job was up to the infantry in spite of the best tank, artillery, and close air support.

It took until the 25th for the regiment to smash through to the outskirts. At midnight, as the final battle for Seoul began, the 5th Marines had the task of slicing through the northwest quarter while the 7th Marines advanced across the northern edge to cut the Seoul-Pyongyang highway. It was up to the 1st Marines on the south to drive straight through the heart of the city, and this regiment met most of the opposition. Three days of deadly street fighting were necessary to reduce road blocks defended by mortars and automatic weapons. Each of these days saw a score of little battles as the Marine tank-infantry-air team slugged ahead from barricade to barricade.

At the height of this struggle, contact was made 25 miles south of Seoul on September 26 between advance forces of the Eighth Army and a 7th Infantry Division regiment of X Corps. This junction, combined with the official liberation of Seoul on the 29th, meant that the NK army was cut off from its best routes of escape across the 38th Parallel. Only the mountain roads of central and east Korea remained as the 1st and 5th Marines fanned out north of Seoul and the 7th Marines fought its way to Uijongbu to block the main highway leading to Pyongyang.

Here the Inchon-Seoul operation ended for the 1st Marine Division on October 7 with its relief by elements of the Eighth Army. Total losses for the three weeks were 417 killed or died of wounds, 1,081 wounded, and five missing. More than two-thirds of these casualties had been incurred in the battle for Seoul and its approaches.

The enemy's losses were 4,972 prisoners and an estimated 13,666 killed and wounded. To this total might be added the loss of the war itself, for events soon proved that the shattered NK army was incapable of recovering without the aid of Red China. And though the possibility of Chinese Communist intervention could not be dismissed, it was not as yet considered an imminent threat in high-level UN military circles. Late in September, therefore, the major units of X Corps were alerted as to planning for a new amphibious operation on the east coast of Korea. It was hoped that this landing, in combination with an Eighth Army drive up the west coast, would end the conflict by stamping out the last embers of organized NK resistance.

Mr. Montross was a student at the University of Nebraska from 1914 to 1917 and a U.S. Army infantryman in France during the next two years. After a newspaper and fiction writing career in New York and Paris, he published *War through the Ages* and two other books of military history. Since 1950 he has been a writer of the Historical Branch, G-3, Headquarters U.S. Marine Corps, specializing in Marine operations in Korea.

8 "Fleet Marine Force Korea—Part II"

Lynn Montross

U.S. Naval Institute *Proceedings*
(September 1953): 995–1005

IT IS NOT OFTEN THAT A LANDING FORCE is called upon for a new amphibious operation before finishing the old one. But this was the experience of the 1st Marine Division while slugging its way through Seoul, two weeks after the Inchon ship-to-shore assault of September 15, 1950. Although another week of hard fighting lay ahead, the Marines and other X Corps major units were warned on the 29th that planning had begun for a new landing at Wonsan on the east coast of Korea.

Five days later an X Corps operational order designated the 1st Marine Division as landing force of TF-90 under the command of Rear Admiral James H. Doyle. When the Leathernecks were relieved north of Seoul on October 7 by Eighth Army elements, it was only to hasten back to Inchon and crowd into the LSTs for the voyage around the peninsula. So rapid was the disintegration of the beaten NK forces, however, that on the 10th Wonsan fell like a ripe plum to the ROKs before the Marines could be outloaded.

High-level Army, Navy, and Marine Corps planners found themselves unable to catch up with a fluid situation. Next they contemplated an X Corps administrative landing at Wonsan on October 20, followed by a drive across the peninsula to combine with the Eighth Army for an attack on Pyongyang. But this prospect faded when the NK capital was taken on the 19th by Eighth Army forces advancing up the west coast.

At least the Red Koreans had learned a belated lesson from Inchon, for the harbor at Wonsan was mined so thoroughly that the Marines were kept on shipboard an additional week while TF-90 cleared a channel. Finally, they began their landing on the 25th, after Bob Hope had already hit the beach to put on a USO show for 1st MAW ground units. It was probably the tamest of the 280 landings in Marine Corps history.

The Marines were assigned a wide variety of blocking and patrolling missions before the arrival of other major X Corps units. These now included the 3d Infantry Division and II ROK Corps (3d and Capital Divisions) as well as the 7th Infantry Division. While the ROKs advanced up the east coast after occupying Wonsan, the Marines had such diverse tasks that the components of the division were soon separated by as much as 118 miles from north to south.

By the first week of November, indeed, it began to appear that the Marine commander, Major General Oliver P. Smith, had to deal with two separate wars. Southwest of Wonsan the 1st Marines was having fire fights with NK guerrillas at Kojo and taking hundreds of prisoners at Majon-ni. Northwest of Hamhung the 7th Marines was engaged meanwhile in the first large-scale American action with the Chinese Communist forces crossing the Yalu to the aid of the beaten Korean Reds.

This regiment, with the largest percentage of reservists in the division, was advancing from Hamhung to Hagaru, at the foot of the Chosin Reservoir, when the collision took place near Chinhung-ni. As a preliminary, the Marines relieved an ROK regiment on November 2 and met scattered Chinese resistance. Then in the early hours of the 3d, bugles and whistles were the signal for an all-out attack by the 124th CCF Division.

It was nip and tuck for a few hours, but the Marines held firm in a perimeter about 6,000 yards long and 2,000 in width. The 1st Battalion occupied the high ground in front; the 3d covered the rear, and the 2d protected the flanks at a distance of 700 to 1,000 yards on either side of the road. Service troops and thin-skinned vehicles remained in the middle, with artillery, mortars, and rocket launchers being disposed around the perimeter for the best effect.

Only a temporary CCF penetration was made during the night fighting. Close air support in the morning enabled the Marines to strengthen their position as air-drops of supplies were received. On the 4th the regiment moved out against a withdrawing enemy. Five T-34 tanks were encountered and four destroyed by a combined Marine air and ground attack. This appears to have been a significant incident, for the Chinese never again used armor against the Marines in northeast Korea.

During the following two days the Marine attack turned into a pursuit of an enemy harassed by the Corsairs. CCF casualties were estimated as high as 9,000 at a cost to the regiment of 46 killed and 264 wounded. And though estimates of enemy losses seldom err on the light side, it is at least certain that the 124th CCF Division was so badly chewed up that it was pulled back into reserve.

The Marines did not find the new enemy more formidable than the best NK troops. Much the same tactical system was employed by both, though the Chinese perhaps showed more skill at night infiltrations. It might appear that Fleet Marine Force training would be wasted in mountain fighting, but perimeter defense has always been emphasized for Marines who might be isolated after a ship-to-shore attack. The 7th Regiment applied these teachings during the advance to Hagaru by retaining at all times a formation able to meet surprise attacks from front, flank, or rear. The four battalions (including an 11th Marines artillery battalion) were in effect a marching fortress by day and a 360° perimeter at night. Patrols usually consisted of company strength and were seldom sent out beyond the reach of protecting artillery fires.

A strange lull now fell over the entire UN front as the Chinese avoided all further contacts while hiding by day and infiltrating through the mountains at night. X Corps had been given the mission of advancing to the

Manchurian border, with the 1st Marine Division on the left, the 7th Infantry Division in the center, II ROK Corps on the right, and the 3d Infantry Division in reserve. Stateside newspapers called it "the race to the Yalu," but the Marine command chose the role of tortoise both as to speed and protection. While a 7th Infantry Division regiment actually reached the Yalu and the ROKs came within a day's march, the Marines were still 125 miles away at Hagaru. Since November 15 they had been busy at strengthening their tenuous line of communications.

The first 35 miles, from Hamhung to Chinhung-ni, were a gradual ascent with a fair road and a narrow-gauge railway. From Chinhung-ni the twisting mountain road climbed 2,400 feet in the ten miles over the hump to Koto-ri, and the next eleven miles to Hagaru were little better than a single-file trail.

This was the MSR on which the eyes of the world would soon be fixed. It was a scene of round-the-clock activity for two weeks as Marine engineers made it fit for tanks and began a C-47 strip at Hagaru. Supply dumps were established at Koto-ri and Hagaru as the 5th Marines followed in the trace of the 7th. Later the three battalions of the 1st arrived to take over the protection of the MSR—1/1 at Chinhung-ni, 2/1 at Koto-ri, and 3/1 at Hagaru.

The division had no more than achieved this relative degree of concentration when Corps orders called for the 5th and 7th Marines to move out in preparation for the combined offensive of Eighth Army in the west and X Corps in the east. The 7th Marines led the 14-mile advance from Hagaru to Yudam-ni, after leaving Fox Company near Sinhung-ni to guard a critical mountain pass. Meanwhile the 5th Marines completed a patrolling mission east of the Reservoir before setting out to join the 7th.

On November 24 a D-day message from General MacArthur announced to X Corps troops that the forthcoming "massive compression envelopment . . . if successful, should for all practicable purposes end the war." But the Chinese struck the ROK right wing of the Eighth Army in overwhelming force the next day and stopped the offensive cold. The long lull was now revealed as a period in which the enemy had been massing his strength in the mountains for this counterstroke.

The Marines pushed ahead about 5,000 yards west of Yudam-ni in response to X Corps orders of November 25 for an effort to relieve the pressure on the Eighth Army. Only a suspiciously light resistance was met until the sub-zero night of the 27th, when the two Marine regiments were attacked by Chinese who had poured into the 80-mile gap between the Eighth Army and X Corps.

Not only the two regiments at Yudam-ni but the entire division was threatened. Eight CCF divisions of about ten thousand men each were employed, including two in reserve. Marine air observation revealed the next morning that they had cut the MSR from Yudam-ni to Hagaru and between that point and Koto-ri.

It is an ironical note that the Chinese generals singled out for destruction the best prepared division of X Corps. Both the 3d and 7th Infantry Divisions were more vulnerable, being widely dispersed and made up largely of green troops. But the enemy elected to fight it out with the one major unit that had been making ready for the worst at a time when overconfidence was a prevailing mood.

In the early hours of the 28th a savage fight took place near Yudam-ni. The 5th and 7th Marines combined their resources, so that unit distinctions meant little. Three battalion sectors were overrun during the night, with only part of the ground being recovered by counterattacks. But the two infantry regiments and three artillery battalions were still holding when Marine air came to their aid in the morning. It had been a costly effort, however, for Yudam-ni losses made up most of the 1,094 Marine casualties reported for November 27 and 28.

The merit of a Marine perimeter defense was demonstrated that night on the company level when Fox Company of the 7th Marines, reinforced by a machine gun section, repulsed the attacks of Chinese in regimental strength. Isolated and surrounded on a hilltop near the Sinhung-ni mountain pass, Captain William E. Barber had a six-hour fight for survival. At dawn the Corsairs finally drove the enemy to cover, and Fox Company received air-drops of supplies and ammunition.

Four tank and infantry patrols, sent out from Hagaru and Koto-ri, had to return after finding their strength inadequate to open the MSR. On the night of the 28th the Hagaru perimeter, containing General Smith's forward CP, was the target of the main CCF effort. This base had to be held at all costs as a division assembly area, but Lieutenant Colonel Thomas L. Ridge, of the 3d Battalion, 1st Marines, had only three combat companies and an assortment of service troops from 24 different units. The Chinese swarmed to the attack in estimated division strength. Marine tanks, howitzers, and mortars could not mow them down fast enough to prevent several positions from being partly overrun. Lacking the numbers to be strong everywhere, Colonel Ridge used his best units to defend the two ridges commanding the half-finished C-47 strip and the village. The enemy threatened several times to smash through by sheer weight, but counterattacks by service troops as well as infantry kept the situation under control. Marine basic training was never more forcibly vindicated than by the efforts of these engineers, clerks, and truck drivers.

The Koto-ri perimeter had its turn that night, but Colonel Puller was loaded for bear when several hundred Chinese launched a night assault. Only 17 got within the Marine lines and none lived to tell the tale. The rest were driven back to the hills, leaving 175 dead behind them.

Fox Company on the hill survived a second all-night battle in spite of the casualties which filled the warming tents. Captain Barber, wounded in the leg, continued to direct the defense, and well-placed artillery fires from Hagaru helped the perimeter to hold out until daybreak brought the Corsairs to the rescue again.

Results of the first 48 hours had demonstrated that Chinese armed with grenades, automatic weapons, and mortars could not prevail against the terrific firepower of a Marine perimeter supported by tactical air and supplied if necessary by air-drop. The CCF troops were masters of camouflage and infiltration; they showed skill and discipline in night operations, and they came on without regard for losses. But these military virtues were offset by a fatal rigidity. Officers apparently had little option below the battalion level; once committed to a tactical pattern, they continued along the same lines until casualties sapped their fighting spirit and cohesion. Their effectiveness, moreover, dwindled from day to day as a consequence of logistical poverty, since they depended for supplies on human or animal transport over the mountains. And though they were warmly clad in padded cotton uniforms, noncombat casualties took a heavy toll as a consequence of meager diet and poor medical care.

If the Chinese could not break through the Marine perimeters, however, neither could the Marines clear the MSR. An attempt was made in battalion strength from Yudam-ni to relieve Fox Company, but it was stopped by heavily defended CCF road blocks. Finally, the urgent need for reinforcements at Hagaru led on the 29th to the most ambitious effort of all. Task Force Drysdale, named after Lieutenant Colonel D. B. Drysdale, commanding the 41st Royal Marine Commando of company size, also included a U.S. Marine and an Army infantry company. Tanks brought up the front and rear to give added protection to the truck convoy of supplies in the middle of the column.

Task Force Drysdale made it about halfway from Koto-ri to Hagaru when the enemy poured down from the hills in estimated regimental strength and caused a halt. CCF mortar shells set several trucks on fire, thus blocking the road and giving the enemy an opportunity to cut the column in two places. The British and U.S. Marines fought their way to Hagaru behind the tanks, and the rear of the column got back to Koto-ri. But the service troops and trucks in the middle were surrounded and compelled to surrender at dawn after exhausting their ammunition in an all-night fight.

As compensation for these losses, the tank and infantry reinforcements which reached Hagaru may have saved that vital perimeter. Nearly 1,500 CCF dead had already been counted, but the enemy came on for the second night against the perilously stretched lines. Fortunately for the Marines, CCF attacks were usually channeled along the same draws or ravines, so that howitzers, 4.2" mortars and 90 mm. tank guns reaped a frightful slaughter. Toward dawn the reinforcements bore the brunt of counterattacks which restored some of the lost positions, and the worst was over at Hagaru.

All five perimeters remained on the defensive another 48 hours, repulsing attacks at Hagaru, Sinhung-ni, and Yudam-ni, which were less violent than those of the first two nights. Then, just before midnight on December 1, the Marines seized the initiative and came out fighting.

The great problem, of course, was one of reuniting a division split into five groups by a more numerous enemy. First, it would be necessary for the two Yudam-ni regiments, burdened with hundreds of casualties, to cut their way to Haguru. And upon them fell the responsibility of relieving Fox Company.

The planning was done jointly by the two regimental commanders and approved by General Smith. It was agreed that the 4,000-foot mountain pass must first be secured and Fox Company relieved. Maneuver seemed out of the question, since only a single road was available. But the planners decided on the bold project of sending a battalion across the trackless mountaintops to take the enemy by surprise.

As a preliminary, a redeployment of the forces at Yudam-ni had to be completed in daylight hours on the 1st, when the Marines could count on air and artillery. The enemy had not mounted an all-out attack since the first night, but this regrouping met heavy opposition. Only superb close air support enabled the two regiments to pull back into a tight new perimeter in readiness for the breakout in the morning.

Darkness had fallen when Lieutenant Colonel Raymond G. Davis and the 1st Battalion of the 7th Marines set out for the Sinhung-ni pass. The temperature dropped to 24 below zero as the wind-whipped Marines stumbled through a wasteland of boulders and snowdrifts. Toward dawn they were staggering with exhaustion when the enemy opened long-distance automatic fire, and the officers found it difficult to rouse them.

Cold and terrain gave more trouble than the enemy, however, and the maneuver succeeded when communication was established with Fox Company in the morning. Just before noon Colonel Davis relieved men who had been isolated five days and nights, and that afternoon he completed his mission by securing the pass.

The Marines at Yudam-ni had pushed out at 0900, led by the single M-26 tank to get that far over the mountain trail. Only wounded men and essential personnel rode the vehicles, and all engineers and artillerymen who could be spared were assigned to rifle companies depleted by losses.

Progress was slow and methodical, averaging about a quarter of a mile per hour. While the point battalion fought its way forward astride of the road, the two flanking battalions secured the high ground on either side until the vehicles passed, then plugged on ahead to repeat the process. When the enemy could not be kept at a safe distance by these means, the column halted and called in air and artillery.

Never was there more daring and effective close air support than that given by 1st MAW planes flying from the fields at Wonsan and Yonpo and from the *Badoeng Strait*. Originally, all air units north of the 38th Parallel were placed under operational control of the 5th Air Force, but on December 2 the responsibility for X Corps tactical support passed to Major General Field Harris, CG 1st MAW. Navy planes of TF-77 were also available for close support, and 5th Air Force planes flew deep support missions beyond a bomb line about five miles on either side of the MSR.

Unusual risks and hardships had to be overcome by the airmen. Flying field runways and carrier decks were glazed with ice, and in the target area the pilot must often dive through or under the overcast at the peril of crashing into a mountainside. Yet in spite of these conditions, the Marine planes alone flew a total of 1,730 sorties from December 1 to 11.

Ground forces along the MSR benefited also from the development of helicopter techniques as a Marine Corps mission dating back to the days of the autogiro. The time was still ten months distant when a Marine battalion and its equipment would be lifted by helicopter in a combat zone.[1] But the "flying windmills" evacuated the most critically wounded from Yudam-ni, and they often made possible the only physical contact between perimeters separated by CCF road blocks.

Altogether, it is a safe assertion that the 5th and 7th Marines might never have made it without Navy, Air Force, and Marine air support of all types. The head of the column reached the Hagaru perimeter at 1900 on December 3 after a 59-hour March, and the rear arrived twenty hours later. All troops were given hot food and taken to warming tents in preparation for a wholesale air evacuation of casualties.

This accomplishment had been made possible by the realistic planning of the Marine command during the "race to the Yalu." The MSR had been strengthened for heavy vehicles, so that dozers and scrapers could be brought up to begin the airstrip at Hagaru. Marine engineers worked day and night under CCF sniper fire, moving the frozen earth. There was time to finish only 2,900 of the 6,000 feet prescribed as "minimum," yet the first C-47 landed without accident on December 1. It took off successfully with 24 wounded Marines, initiating an evacuation in which only one plane crashed and no lives or casualties were lost.

The very military situation hinged on the outcome, since the 1st Marine Division could not fight its way from Hagaru to the seacoast while burdened with hundreds of casualties. More than 2,000 of them had to be evacuated from that perimeter in three days to make room for the 2,400 casualties expected from Yudam-ni as walking wounded or riders on vehicles.

This was the problem confronting Captain E. R. Hering (MC), USN, division surgeon, and the Navy medical officers and corpsmen attached to the division. Fortunately, they were prepared for the emergency. The amphibious mission of the Marines calls for a close integration of military surgery with combat tactics, since a landing force may be isolated without the usual facilities for evacuating its wounded. New techniques had already been tested during the Inchon landing, when specially trained surgical teams hit the beaches in the trace of the first waves and operated on seriously wounded men in the LSTs without a single death resulting after major surgery.

At Hagaru these specialists managed in 48 hours to empty the hospital tents of helpless cases and evacuate them on the C-47s or R4Ds to the hospital ship *Consolation* at Hungnam, the division hospital at Hamhung, and base hospitals in Japan. Among them were more than a thousand casualties from three 7th Infantry Division battalions cut off east of the Reservoir and badly mauled by the enemy. Marine volunteers led by Lieutenant Colonel Olin L. Beall crossed the ice of the Reservoir on jeeps and sleds under enemy fire to bring in helpless soldiers. About 450 unhurt survivors were issued Marine equipment at Hagaru and formed into a provisional battalion. This was in accordance with X Corps orders of November 30 placing General Smith in operational control of all Army as well as Marine forces in the Reservoir area.

So far the breakout of the 1st Marine Division had proceeded according to plan. The first phase was the attack from Yudam-ni to Hagaru, and the second consisted of the defense of Hagaru. Next came the move from Hagaru to Koto-ri, and the period from December 2 to 6 was devoted to intensive preparations for this third phase. Evacuation of casualties continued until a total of 4,675 were flown out from Hagaru and another improvised airstrip at Koto-ri. Ammunition and supplies were being airdropped to both perimeters meanwhile by the C-119s of the Combat Cargo Command of the Fifth Air Force in Japan.

The logistical situation might have been more serious if the Marine command had not provided a reserve, while the MSR was still open, of two units of fire and six days' rations. Even so, a total of 1,949 tons of supplies was requested by air-drop, with the Hagaru perimeter alone calling for such quantities as 1,466,740 rounds of small arms ammunition, 2,160 rounds of 105 mm. howitzer, 15,168 rounds of 60 mm. mortar, and 11,660 gallons of gasoline. Not all of these amounts could be delivered, and air-drop losses from breakage or misdirection were considerable.

Enough supplies were received, however, for the division to initiate its attack from Hagaru to Koto-ri on December 6. Just before daybreak the 7th Marines moved out as the artillery placed heavy concentrations of 105 mm. fire along the route ahead. The plan called for this regiment to lead the advance while the 5th Marines defended Hagaru and the rear of the vehicle column. Again the key terrain features on both sides of the road were first to be secured by infantry clearing both flanks ahead of the vehicles. But since the rear of the column would just be leaving Hagaru when the head entered Koto-ri, it was obviously impossible to provide complete security. Sometimes the enemy was swept back by the Marine infantry, only to pour down from the hills again for renewed efforts. One of these flank attacks struck a battalion of the 11th Marines on the night of the 6th, and the gunners had to double as infantry while delivering artillery fire at ranges of 40 to 500 yards.

The 5th Marines covered the withdrawal to Haragu all day on the 6th, and heavy attacks on the perimeter were repulsed that night. Effective air cover enabled the regiment to complete its own withdrawal the following morning, but hard fights awaited along the route before the last units reached Koto-ri at dark on the 7th. Targets of the supporting aircraft were often only a hundred yards ahead of the troops, with the Corsairs swooping so low that the mortarmen had the problem of lobbing their 81 mm. shells between the attacking planes. A total of 201 sorties in close support of ground troops was flown by the 1st MAW during the two critical days.

Next came the fourth and final phase of the breakout—ten miles "over the hump" from Koto-ri to Chinhung-ni at the foot of the mountains. This area was believed to be the most likely of all for a decisive CCF attack, and once more the plans called for the infantry to move out ahead of the vehicle train and secure key terrain features on both flanks. All major units of the division were now united with the exception of the 1st Battalion of the 1st Marines at Chinhung-ni which was given the mission of covering the last stage of the withdrawal. After being relieved by

TF Dog, a reinforced battalion of the 3d Infantry Division, the Marines attacked northward in a blinding snowstorm to seize ridge lines commanding the route of the main column moving southward.

Visibility was limited at times to six feet as the battalion fought until nightfall on the 8th against mounting resistance, then dug in to resume the action at daybreak. Marine engineers had the task meanwhile of installing sections of a 24-ton Treadway bridge, air-dropped by the C-119s, at a point where the route could not be bypassed. While this was being accomplished, the 1st Battalion of the 1st Marines secured and defended its objectives so ably that the head of the division column entered Chinhung-ni that night. Little resistance was encountered after leaving the mountains behind, and the 13-day Reservoir operation ended on December 11 with the Marines safe in the warming tents of Hamhung.

Not only had the division fought its way through eight Chinese divisions; it had brought out most of its arms and equipment, and it had brought out the survivors of the three Army battalions cut off in the Reservoir area. And though a total of 7,350 Marine casualties had been suffered, they included 3,655 nonbattle casualties consisting chiefly of frostbite cases soon restored to active duty. Enemy losses were estimated at 25,000 killed and 12,500 wounded, and it appeared likely that more thousands had perished or had been incapacitated by freezing or privations.

Events soon proved that the 1st Marine Division had done more than extricate itself from a trap. It had rendered militarily ineffective the 9th CCF Army Group, numbering 12 divisions, which might have turned the retreat of the Eighth Army into a catastrophe if they could have been shifted to west Korea. Finally, the Marines had made possible the redeployment of X Corps by sea without serious interference from the remnants of these CCF divisions.

High-level planners decided on this evacuation during the Eighth Army withdrawal to a line south of the 38th Parallel, thus exposing the entire left flank of X Corps. The redeployment of five X Corps divisions from Hungnam, aptly called "an amphibious operation in reverse," was completed from December 10 to 24 by TF-90, commanded by Admiral Doyle. Navy and Marine officers planned the details in a few days, and Marine shore party elements had charge of the outloading. Meanwhile the enemy was kept at a respectful distance by naval gunfire and Navy, Marine, and Air Force planes, so that the ground forces had only a few minor clashes with an enemy numerous enough to have launched a major attack.

Altogether, TF-90 evacuated about 100,000 troops, 90,000 Korean civilian refugees, 17,500 vehicles, and 350,000 measurement tons of cargo in two December weeks. A more convincing demonstration of sea power has seldom been recorded.

The Marine Division, as the first major unit to embark, landed at Pusan for redeployment in an assembly area near Masan. General Walker was killed in a jeep accident late in December, and Lieutenant General Matthew B. Ridgway took command of the Eighth Army only a few days before a second Chinese offensive exploded in the bitter cold of New Year's Eve. Outweighed UN forces were compelled to evacuate Seoul and pull back by January 10 to a prepared line that represented UN withdrawals of about 200 miles since November 25.

This is one of the few historical instances of Marines having no part in a great battle. The 1st Marine Division, much depleted by casualties, recuperated in the Masan area while training the first arrivals of 3,387 replacements. Then on January 10, after passing from X Corps into Eighth Army reserve, the division was given the mission of neutralizing a North Korean guerrilla division that had infiltrated through UN lines into the Pohang-Andong area of southeast Korea. About 1,600 square miles were contained in the new sector, which offered some knotty problems in transport and supply as well as reconnaissance. But the Marines carried out their mission so effectively that General Smith reported to CG Eighth Army on February 6 an estimated reduction of 60 percent in the strength of an enemy division originally estimated at 6,000 to 8,000 troops. This result owed largely to the self-sufficient Marine "rice paddy patrols" which combed the wildly mountainous sector on foot. Helicopter tactics also received a new impetus, with those aircraft being freely used for supply and evacuation as well as reconnaissance.

A turning point was reached in February, when CG Eighth Army requested General Smith to submit recommendations for the future employment of his division. The Marine general, after staff consultations, replied that he favored the commitment of his troops to an east coast sector, where they would be readily available if future developments created the opening for a new amphibious landing. General Ridgway concurred at first, but intelligence of a large-scale CCF offensive build-up caused him to summon General Smith to Taegu on February 12 to confer on using the Marines in the line on the central front. The Eighth Army commander recognized the advantages of utilizing Marine amphibious training and experience, but he asserted that he needed "the most powerful division in Korea" in a sector that appeared to be the logical corridor for a new CCF drive.

On February 21, therefore, the 1st Marine Division jumped off north of Chungju to spearhead the IX Corps advance in Operation KILLER. This was one of the limited objective offensives mounted by General Ridgway in the spring of 1951 to keep the enemy off balance and break up preparations for a great new CCF offensive. After securing all objectives on schedule, the Marines led the IX Corps advance in Operation RIPPER from March 7 to 26, taking Hongchon and Chunchon while driving to the 38th Parallel.

Further UN gains were made in April as General Ridgway continued to prod the enemy, and not until the 22d could the Chinese begin their long expected offensive. The early retirement of an ROK division stripped the entire left flank of the Marines in the Hwachon Reservoir area, but they faced west as well as north to beat off all attacks with heavy losses.

Soon the elastic defense strategy of the Eighth Army proved so effective that the Chinese had only empty territorial gains to show for frightful personnel losses. They tried again on May 16 and the Marines helped to restore the situation in an adjacent sector after local CCF penetrations in east Korea. The Eighth Army seized the initiative before the enemy could lick his wounds, and UN forces were advancing in the early summer of 1951 when the first peace talks brought a lull.

Thus the first year of the Marines in Korea ended tamely, in X Corps reserve, with minor patrol actions and training exercises in assembly areas of east Korea. It was virtually a new 1st Marine Division by this time, since replacements had largely taken over during the last six months from "rotated" veterans of Inchon-Seoul and the Reservoir. Not only had these newcomers been hardened in combat, but the division had trained a fourth infantry regiment made up wholly of Korean Marine Corps (KMC) troops. Under the "buddy system" Korean soldiers had been taken into a number of U.S. Army regiments, but the Marines favored a policy of setting up special units imbued with a high *esprit de corps*. Two KMC battalions fought well in the attack on Seoul, and in March 1951, the 1st KMC Regiment began a participation with the 1st Marine Division which continued creditably throughout the rest of the year.

A review of the first twelve months of the division in Korea might seem to indicate that its amphibious mission had been largely wasted in infantry operations of mountain warfare. Yet the results go far toward proving that the advantages of Fleet Marine Force doctrine and training are not limited to ship-to-shore attacks. For the potential dangers and difficulties of an amphibious landing call for highly trained skills which have their uses in any military situation demanding the utmost in power and precision. Thus while Inchon-Seoul showed what amphibious specialists could do when sticking to their own tactical trade, the Reservoir demonstrated that amphibious training also scored in the frozen mountains of northeast Korea. The desirability of using Marines for such tasks may be questioned, but there can be no doubt about their competence.

As the scope of Communist ambitions revealed itself after World War II, it became a popular belief that aggression would take the form of huge armies emerging ponderously from behind the Iron Curtain with earthshaking columns of tanks and guns. It was even urged here and there by professional soldiers that the best if not the only defense lay in preparation for the pachydermous tactics of continental land-mass warfare. But while such theories were being advocated, the enemy actually struck. And instead of using mastodon tactics, the enemy resorted to the old totalitarian politico-military dodge of secretly arming "oppressed" peoples with nationalist aspirations.

The Dutch East Indies and French Indo-China were first. Then came Korea and a first year's experience demonstrated the uses of amphibious techniques and the tactics of small, self-contained units as compared to land mass warfare.

Mobility has been more effective than mass on this somber Asiatic peninsula, where results depend so much on close coordination of land and sea forces. And though the possibility of a large-scale invasion of Europe can never be dismissed, the world's headlines speak more ominously of made-to-order political discontent in lands of Asia and Africa. Meanwhile the lesson of Korea has been neatly even if indirectly summed up by General J. Lawton Collins. chief of staff of the U.S. Army:

"Only one military organization can hold and gain ground in war—a ground army supported by tactical aviation and with supply lines guarded by a navy."

General Collins, of course, meant this statement in a broad and general sense. But it would be hard to find a more forceful specific illustration than the results achieved by the 1st Marine Division and the 1st Marine Aircraft Wing together with U.S. Navy task forces in Korea.

Note
1. The 1st Marine Division made tactical history in September and October 1951, with a series of helicopter operations culminating in the lift of a battalion in a sector of east Korea.

"Number Five"

9

Lieutenant Commander Thomas J. Cutler,
USN (Ret.)

U.S. Naval Institute *Proceedings*
(June 2014): 93

SINCE THE SURPRISE ASSAULT at Inchon in September 1950, the
North Korean Army was in a northward retreat. United Nations forces
had not only regained lost South Korean territory but were pushing farther up the peninsula, closing in on what seemed certain victory. But on
25 October, Chinese communist forces entered the war, pouring across
the border in overwhelming numbers.

The situation rapidly deteriorated, and many U.N. units found themselves in serious trouble. Among those was the 1st Marine Division, then
commanded by Major General O. P. Smith and located near a reservoir
in northeast Korea known to the Koreans as "Changjin." Because the
Marines were relying on older Japanese maps that called the reservoir
"Chosin," that name found its way into the history books.

Surrounded, these Marines alternately attacked enemy territory and
defended their own for several days while enduring incredibly harsh
winter conditions that included temperatures of 20 degrees below zero.
Casualties included a number of intestinal problems caused by eating
frozen C-rations.

When the time came to fight their way out and return to the sea at
the port of Hungnam, General Smith refused to call the action a retreat,

referring to it instead as an "attack to the rear." With six squadrons of Marine Corsairs providing air cover, some 14,000 men and more than 1,000 vehicles formed a procession that stretched more than 11 miles.

Forming the rear guard were two battalions commanded by Colonel Lewis B. "Chesty" Puller, whose courage under fire was already legendary. Having missed the fighting in World War I despite his efforts to participate, Puller made up for that disappointment by seeing action in Haiti and Nicaragua before landing at Guadalcanal in World War II, where he saw heavy combat and earned a number of decorations. In subsequent battles, including the meat grinder at Peleliu—one of the bloodiest battles in Marine Corps history—Puller's reputation as a tenacious, courageous leader was well established.

He lived up to his colorful reputation in Korea, first during the Inchon landing, where he earned a Silver Star, and then in the Chosin action. Encouraging the Marines with his personal example and with his words, he urged them on despite hellacious combat and horrific weather conditions. Coming from him, words like "You're the 1st Marine Division and don't you forget it" were more than mere bravado. When he told the Marines, "We're the greatest military outfit that ever walked on this earth," few, if any, doubted him. And his words proved prophetic as well as inspiring, when he said, "Not all the communists in Hell can stop you. We'll go down to the sea at our own pace and nothing is going to get in our way. If it does, we'll blow hell out of it."

And down to the sea they indeed went. When this "attack to the rear" was complete, the Marines had lost 718 men killed in action. Intelligence estimates numbered the Chinese dead at more than 25,000—coupled with their wounded, an attrition rate of more than 50 percent. In subzero winter conditions, the Marines had destroyed no less than seven divisions of the Chinese Ninth Army Group, and had provided the Corps and the nation with a much-needed morale boost in those dark days when a certain victory was suddenly transformed into a major setback that would portend a long and frustrating continuation of the war.

For his actions at Chosin, Chesty Puller was awarded the Navy Cross, an impressive achievement under any circumstances, made all the more remarkable by the fact that it was his fifth—a record that still stands to this day.

Lieutenant Commander Cutler is the author of several Naval Institute Press books, including *A Sailor's History of the U.S. Navy* and *Brown Water, Black Berets.*

10 "The Snowy Battle for Hill 1304"

Captain William J. Davis, USMC

Naval History (December 2010): 24–26

NOTE: *At dawn on 8 December 1950, around 14,000 Marines, U.S. Soldiers, Royal Marine Commandos, and South Korean Police were crowded into the hamlet of Koto-ri, North Korea, in preparation for the next stage of their march south from the Chosin Reservoir. The 7th Marines, reinforced with the Provisional Army Battalion, were to lead the day's advance, seizing the heights bordering the main supply route (MSR) where it began winding down through the Funchilin Pass to Chinhung-ni. Trucks carrying air-dropped treadway bridge sections to span the route's destroyed bridge within the pass were to follow closely behind the regiment. The 1st Battalion, 1st Marines would meanwhile move north from Chinhung-ni to capture Hill 1081, which dominated the MSR in the pass. The converging forces met at the blown bridge on 9 December, and that evening vehicles began rolling over the treadway span.*

What follows is an edited version of then–first lieutenant William J. Davis' account of 8 December and his company's role in seizing and then holding Hill 1304 at the head of Funchilin Pass. Davis' original article appeared in the July 1953 issue of Naval History's *sister publication,* Proceedings.

THE 1ST MARINE DIVISION in Korea is built around three infantry regiments, the 1st, 5th, and 7th Marines. We of the 7th Marines were to be the "point" of the last drive from Koto-ri down through the Funchilin Pass to Chinhung-ni, and there, we had heard, was freedom—or at least relative freedom.

Since the 7th had three battalions—the 1st, 2d, and 3d—naturally the lineup would be numerical. And since the 1st Battalion had three rifle companies—A, B, and C—naturally, here it would be alphabetical. That wasn't too bad, because we in Able Company, as the Point, would get to walk on the level ground for a short while. They gave us two tanks in support at dawn, and we were off.[1]

It wasn't a bad day, in fact, the sun tried to shine. However, from the very first that morning, I got the funny feeling that something strange was about to happen.

To get a picture of our road, just think of the best highway you can, then imagine it in the worst possible condition, beginning with a width of about ten yards at best down to five yards as an average, and edged by 50 yards of rocks or rice paddy fields and then hills that grew up to be mountains within 150 yards of the road.

Take a couple of hundred huge green parkas, place camouflaged-covered helmets on top of them, give them rifles, carbines (no—you can keep your damn carbines), mortars, light machine guns, and there we are, out on an early morning stroll. We've been doing it for a couple of months now, and we're starting to get in shape. Things are quiet, and we're all daydreaming except when C Company on our right sees a few Chinese on the skyline—a rare sight, usually it's just Marines crazy enough for that—and the tanks throw a few 90-mm rounds up into 'em for reveille purposes, and we continue on.

All in all, it's pretty quiet; the Chinese aren't throwing in any artillery or mortar rounds as they did on our treks back from Yudam-ni to Hagaru-ri and then again to Kotori. And the thought that we all know that if we don't run into too much today, we should be down through the pass tomorrow kind of helps the day move along.

Then the thing we had all prayed against during the whole trip down—SNOW! And what snow! And with it came lightning—yes, the manmade lightning of lead flashing across the sky.

We hadn't gone 100 yards when we hit a frozen stream about 25 yards wide. The first three men to dash across the ice made it, but the fourth was cut in half by automatic fire that sounded about 300 yards up the stream to our right.

The field on the left side of the road was about 3 feet below the road level, so a man who ran at a crouch had a pretty fair defilade. All we needed was a little clearing of the skies, and we could call up our equalizers—air and artillery. I stood in the ditch and tried to look across the road, but no dice. I could see less than 50 yards, and there were no Chinese in sight and no Charlie Company.

A quick radio buzz showed that C Company was holding up, hoping for a break in the snow. Its men could hear automatic weapons to their front but could see nothing but snow, and their artillery forward observer (FO) was going berserk trying to get an estimate of range for his battery of 105s. Normally a quick pass by a Corsair or two or a few artillery rounds and this bottleneck would be no strain. But here the Chinese had us—temporarily. We couldn't see them, but they knew where we had to come, because our wounded had to be on vehicles that had to be on the road. Thus they used this bridge and river bottleneck for a well-chosen roadblock.

Well, snow or no snow, we couldn't stay here long. We had to keep driving forward. Up limped the battalion commander, who had been hit in the foot farther back but refused to be evacuated by plane.[2] A glimpse at him and we forgot our own troubles. He looked over the situation and had it solved in a matter of moments. Baker Company would move along our side of the road, and take the high ground our maps showed 250 yards to our left front. Able Company could stay close to the road for

150 yards and then cut across the road to the high ground on the right from which our point was now receiving heavy automatic fire. Then Charlie Company would move out and hit the same piece of terrain from Abie's right flank.

We passed the word to our troops and after a fast cigarette or a chomp on an old cigar, the now-second nature "Move out!" was hardly needed as we started again. The lead platoon had crossed the river with only two casualties when suddenly the Chinese really started blazing. They had us pretty badly pinned down, but only momentarily because we finally got a five-minute break. The snow slowed down to a trot, and we could see through for a good 200 yards. The men in the lead platoon were up en masse with a yell, and they blasted Chinese in all directions.

Over to our right flank was an open valley a good 500 yards long. We could see a single column of at least 250 Chinese slowly filing along toward the high ground Able was slated to take. As the tanks roared up and commenced saturating the valley with .50-caliber slugs, the first artillery white-phosphorous shell landed 50 yards to the left of the column. No strain now—we had 'em cold!

But then the sky dropped to the deck as the rumble of the 105s sounded back in Koto-ri, and we didn't see another round. The whole thing was like a bad dream. At the same moment, one of our new rifle platoon lieutenants was shot when he was actually in defilade.[3]

He was racing in a crouch up to his point when some Chinese sprayed the road haphazardly. The enemy couldn't have seen his target, but the round found its mark. One—it only takes one—hit a rock on the edge of the road on our side and tore a jagged hole in his parka and his heart, and before we could yell for our last corpsman, he was no longer with us. His platoon sergeant looked pretty badly shaken up for a moment, but he had his men take a quick look, single file, and then they charged up over the road and across it into this rice paddy valley.

They headed for the high ground paralleling the road about 50 yards on the right. By now the Chinese were aware of our moving up. They were throwing fire in all directions, and hand grenades were punctuating the sound of their automatic weapons.

As our point started up to the high ground, the snow slowed down for another five-minute break, and that's all we needed. The hillside seemed alive with men's arms—every Chinese in the world was throwing hand grenades! These concussion grenades bark big and bite small, usually. And in a moment their throwers were panicky.

Apparently, they expected a few casualties to turn the whole company back (the company was one in spirit only—we started with 227 men, now had 36), but they were slightly confused when they caught a couple of dozen M-1s firing eight rounds each semi-automatic. They seemed to forget they had fully automatic weapons of their own. We reached the top of this square summit that measured about 50 yards on all sides, just as the Chinese reinforcements filing in from the west arrived. Well-placed machine-gun and mortar rounds cut their Mao Tse-tungian banzai into rice-like pieces, and our riflemen rolled grenades down on 'em for a little further discouragement.

As our most hated enemy, darkness, stifled us, we pulled our numerically meager troops back about 15 yards from the perimeter and passed the word to shoot the Chinese as they charged over the crest of the hill. This worked well, because our prayers stopped the falling snow, and the khaki-covered enemy made a beautiful contrast with the bright snowy deck. They rushed time and time again throughout the night, but good, slightly frozen Marine fingers on good M-1s picked them off like targets on a stateside rifle range. With the clearing of the skies, our artillery FOs started their radios buzzing and the situation was no longer in doubt.

To me, this was the turning point in our breakout. We now had the high ground at the top of the pass above Chinghung-ni, the 1st Battalion, 1st Marines was on its way clearing a path up from the bottom of the pass, and our so-called "withdrawal" was just a matter of time now.

The Chinese had had their chance and muffed it, or, more accurately, we muffed it for them. We moved on to the pass itself at dawn, met the

1st Battalion, and it was relatively all over but the shouting—which we were too cold and tired to accomplish. I only hope that we who were fortunate enough to survive this breakout will ever be blessed with the privilege of upholding the honor of these men among men—the chosen Marines of the Chosin Reservoir—the "Cold Breed."

Notes

1. The two tanks were likely the pair assigned to the Provisional Army Battalion. Other tanks were to follow the vehicular column so if one was destroyed it would not block other traffic.
2. The 1st Battalion, 7th Marines' commander was MAJ Webb Sawyer. Though wounded two days earlier while serving as executive officer of the regiment's 2d Battalion, Sawyer had taken over the 1st Battalion after its commander was promoted to regimental XO.
3. 1LT Leslie C. Williams.

" '...and a Few Marines' "

11

*Lieutenant Colonel William G.
Leftwich Jr., USMC*

U.S. Naval Institute *Proceedings*
(August 1968): 34–45

THE FOREIGN OFFICER in the unfamiliar uniform stood before the ill-equipped soldiery and, lacking a facility in the mother tongue of the troops, he took a weapon in hand and painstakingly demonstrated each of the movements he sought to convey. When he called upon his pupils to imitate, total confusion ensued, accompanied by torrents of laughter. The professional endured stoically for a few minutes, and then exploded: "Goddam de gaucheries of dese badauts. Je ne puis plus. I can curse dem no more."

Thus did Baron Frederick William von Steuben, an early military advisor, begin the celebrated reorganization of the Continental Army. He successfully communicated his desires through the techniques of pantomime and mimicry and captured the affections of his hosts with an inspired bit of multilingual psychology. Few more effective advisory efforts have been recorded in history, although the concept is as ancient as the profession of arms.

The U.S. Marine Corps was not to enter the advisory sphere until 1915, when Major Smedley D. Butler undertook the training of a native Haitian Gendarmerie.

There were various other ventures in the advisory field, but not until World War II did the United States find itself projected into relationships that girdled the globe. Virtually all of these took the form of liaison or technical instruction in the use of American equipment, except in two notable cases, Iran and China. Here, advisors actually commanded on occasion, but more importantly, they shaped the counterpart system and extended its purview to operations as well as logistics and training.

Wartime commitments and the rising specter of Communist imperialism led to an extension of advisory efforts as the war ended and the Iron Curtain descended. In response to the Truman Doctrine, Congress detailed troops to Greece in 1947 to serve in "an advisory capacity only." The Military Assistance Program as we know it today is considered to have dated from this legislation.

The pattern of duties within the assorted MAAGs, JUSMAGs, MAGs, and Missions, as they have been variously known, differed from country to country, but generally followed a line of advice in organizational and logistical areas, spilling over into operations or even command when active combat threatened, as it did in Korea in 1950. The early 1950s also brought into common usage the term "country team," which was applied to the relationship between military and economic aid agencies at work in the same country.

Marine Corps contributions to these various commitments were minimal, primarily limited to naval attaches, until 1951 when advisors were assigned to both the fledgling Korean and Chinese Marine Corps. The fruits of 14 years of Korean advisory efforts were realized when the Blue Dragon Brigade stepped ashore in Vietnam in 1965 to face another Communist enemy.

The pattern of aggression that provoked the commitments represented by these various advisory groups has evolved with sinister efficiency. Thwarted by nuclear standoff after World War II, international Communism reverted to its historic tactics of subversion. The most militant practitioners since 1945 have been the Red Chinese, rather than the

Soviets and Mao Tse-tung has become the insurgent's reigning prophet. So acknowledged is Mao as the chief architect of what Khrushchev first termed "wars of national liberation" that his maxims have been incorporated outright into U.S. counterinsurgency doctrine. Joint Chiefs Publication One defines the threat of insurgency in its several gradations as: "A condition resulting from revolt or insurrection against a constituted government which falls short of civil war." In precise parody of Mao the various levels of intensity of insurgency are further delineated: "Phase I, Latent and Incipient Subversion; Phase II, Organized Guerrilla Warfare; and Phase III, A War of Movement."

This insidious design and the range of U.S. responses have collided in South Vietnam. This unhappy land provides the laboratory for a classic experiment in counterinsurgency and a classic test tube for the advisory concept.

The U.S. advisory era began undramatically on 29 September 1954, with the arrival of a Military Assistance and Advisory Group (MAAG). As the French departed, the MAAG began what might be called the purely advisory phase of its involvement. Two other phases would follow, integration of combat support elements, and liaison, each adding new dimensions to the advisory mission.

Meanwhile, the victorious Viet Minh, having climaxed Mao's three phases of insurgent warfare with a decisive defeat of the French at Dien Bien Phu, reverted once more to Phase I. In defiance of treaty obligations to withdraw north of the 17th parallel, Communist military and political cadres remained in the south to exploit the general distress. Until 1957, their efforts would be largely psychological and unarmed.

MAAG's concept for employment of the new Army of the Republic of Vietnam (ARVN) envisioned resistance to conventional invasion across the 17th parallel in the manner of Korea until treaty forces could arrive. Accordingly, reorganization proceeded along standard U.S. Army lines, a philosophy which the late author Bernard B. Fall disparaged as "the American type war we train for and the Indo-China war we will have to fight."

The advisory function in this period was the traditional one of counsel, but not command. Advisor purview extended into all areas, but their numbers were limited, and primary emphasis was on reorganization and training. Marine participation at this time was limited to an assistant naval attaché and a single advisor to the fledgling Vietnamese Marine Corps, which evolved from the French Commando groups in 1954.

The leisurely training pace quickened into an increasingly operational one when the Communists, now called Viet Cong, stepped up the tempo of subversive activity in 1959. By 1961, Mao's vaunted Phase II, with its guerrilla attacks, was again in progress, and President John F. Kennedy directed a substantial build-up in December. In the year that followed, the number of advisors increased from 1,364 to 9,865, and the Military Assistance Command Vietnam (MACV) superseded the MAAG as administrators of the vastly augmented U.S. effort.

Coincident with the influx of advisors was an increase in the Marine Corps contingent, permitting the assignment of a single advisor to each of the now five Vietnamese Marine battalions. These young officers were immediately plunged into a combat operational role that limited but did not obviate the training function. On a one-year tour without dependents, they would spend 32 per cent of 1962 in the field.

The same year ushered in a new phase in the advisory effort, the control of U.S. combat support elements. This evolution was precipitated by the introduction of two helicopter units; one Army and one Marine. Their arrival brought to the experimental arena the fragile machines that have become the very symbol of the counterinsurgency effort. The mission of these now famous "Hueys" and H-34s was direct combat support of Vietnamese forces, but only American advisors could approve their employment and control their disposition.

The advisor was compelled to broaden his range of skills. He was now a forward air controller as well as a ground operational and training advisor. The close co-ordination required made him essentially a commander during helicopter assaults. As one advisor described it: "I was in charge until we reached the treeline." He was also in the midst of a very real war. The first of the advisory legion fell in combat only a week after President Kennedy's historic directive of December 1961; and in April 1963, the Army would make it official by approving the award of the Combat Infantryman's Badge.

U.S. military advisors contributed construction advice to the "Strategic Hamlet" concept, and their military efforts were further expanded to include the training of paramilitary Popular and Regional Forces as well as the ARVN. These innovations represented the first advisory ventures into the sphere known as nation-building. In two more years, Army advisors would be assigned as district and province advisors with specific responsibilities in the civilian as well as the military realm.

Marine Corps participation increased proportionately as the Viet Cong Phase II intensified. "On-the-job trainees" spent one- month tours with the Marine Advisory Group, officers joined the MACV staff, and in 1964 officers and NCOs began filling ARVN advisory billets in the I Corps area.

Advisors during the 1961–1965 period played out a colorful and demanding role. A correspondent depicted the advisory crusade as "a wonderfully American invention, idealistic and romantic in the Lawrence of Arabia mold, and basically unworkable." Indeed, this period recaptured for a new generation a measure of the appeal the Lafayette Escadrille provided an earlier one. Theirs was a multifaceted endeavor accentuated by a backdrop of increasing combat intensity. Vietnamese Marine battalions by 1964 were spending 83 per cent of their time in combat operations.

Always foremost and most trying among the advisor's concerns was that of pure counselling. Field advisors were junior in rank to the commanders with whom they worked, and generally less experienced professionally. They had no command authority whatsoever and exerted only the influence their powers of persuasion might work, while suffering the same degree of risk as their counterparts. Indeed, their physical size and peculiar function made them a more frequent target. They were compelled to adjust immediately to the unfamiliar cultural patterns of a totally foreign environment and were required to communicate with great subtlety through the unsubtle medium of sign language and pidgin English. One correspondent summed up his situation: "Our man in charge on the ground with no real say in what happened but with responsibility to make it happen well."

While the rendering of advice was a paramount concern, co-ordination of U.S. assets was an increasingly demanding process that dominated the advisor's time and energies during the actual course of operations. By early 1965, American pilots were also flying U.S. fixed-wing aircraft in close support, reconnaissance, and logistical roles. Helicopter support was augmented to the extent of providing virtually all the evacuation, liaison, and combat lift requirements. The middleman for these multiple agencies remained the advisor, who now held the means to influence critically the course of action—if he used them properly. Countless "After Action Reports" attest the abilities of advisors to do just this with often decisive results.

The third and final dimension in this phase of the advisory experiment was added in early 1965. This was the requirement for liaison with U.S. operational units. The Communist insurgency is generally regarded to have reached Phase III proportions at the Battle of Binh Gia on the last day of 1964. A series of other setbacks at the hands of conventionally equipped and operating enemy elements compelled the dispatch of U.S. forces shortly thereafter and ushered in the liaison era. This new challenge demanded advisor dexterity with the radio and placed an increasing reliance on rapport with his Vietnamese counterpart. Now the advisor was required to speak with new and unimpeachable authority on the details of zones of operation, fire responsibilities, and patrol areas. The sometimes loose co-ordination of adjacent Vietnamese units was supplanted by the customary precise definition of U.S. practice. New stress lay also on the advisor's grasp of local intelligence with its special value to American units which were arriving in profusion by the summer of 1965.

Co-ordination with U.S. units brought ever-increasing firepower and added artillery and naval gunfire to the advisor's fire control considerations. Illustrative was an operation in which advisors called fire missions for their counterparts, Vietnamese spotted in Vietnamese to be translated by advisors at the battery position, and counterparts directed fire in pidgin English.

The age of combined operations—another key ingredient in the counterinsurgency lab—was inaugurated for Marines in the fall of 1965. In Operation "Blue Marlin" in November, Vietnamese and U.S. Marines were on adjacent beaches for the first time in history. Among the liaison aspects of the venture was the housing and feeding, on board U.S. ships, of Vietnamese Marines accustomed to squad cooking fires and slapdash sanitation. The much-beset advisory structure once more provided the medium for successful resolution. That this liaison talent has continued is reflected in Pulitzer Prize Winner Peter Arnette's comment late in 1967: "The U.S. and Vietnamese Marines are working together in an ideal arrangement . . . one not enjoyed elsewhere in the country."

Thus, today, after 14 years of representation in South Vietnam, the advisor performs three functions. He is at once a counsellor to a foreign force with unrestricted purview in the military field, a technical manipulator of multiple U.S. assets, and a jack-of-all-trades liaison officer. The first and last of these are historic advisor duties; the second is a product of this test tube war.

These tasks have accrued consecutively, but unevenly. Officers originally assigned to billets envisaged as conventional training ones were required to adapt immediately to combat advising and then to counterinsurgency emphasis. The arrival of U.S. support elements necessitated the diversion of attention and energies to purely mechanical control techniques. On the part of the average advisor these fluctuations required innovation and self-teaching on the job. Liaison tasks were an extension of the support function, but depended heavily on an instinctive knowledge of the advised unit, its commander, and its capabilities.

An evaluation of the advisory effort since its introduction in the Vietnam experiment would seem to reflect failure in that advisory measures alone failed to halt the spread of insurgency for the second time in two decades. The ultimate issue remains to be determined, however. The fact that the present intensity of advisory effort was not attained until 1965, when Phase III insurgency was already in progress, precludes a common perspective from which to analyze relative results. Had the Vietnamese armed services been trained for counterinsurgency by advisors down to battalion level throughout the period 1955–1961, the current situation might be altogether different. Instead, emphasis did not shift from conventional directions until 1961 and then only in spasmodic sequence. Most Vietnamese units did not see an advisor until they were committed to combat, and training opportunities were thus much reduced. Consequently, advisors with no participation in the training cycle have had to discern shortcomings in the field and find themselves struggling to sustain current operations rather than enhancing future capabilities.

Still there have been definite achievements during the advisory era. Major General William E. DePuy, MACV's J-3 in 1965, wrote: "Had we not had advisors with Vietnamese units they would have collapsed completely in May, June, and July of 1965. If we didn't have the advisory system, we would have had to create it."

Selecting and training the advisor. While the priorities of the three advisory functions may vary, there is general agreement that all three hinge on an intangible: the advisor's relationship with his opposite number. The vital need, then, is rapport between an advisor who has more formal education, but less rank, and generally much less counterinsurgency experience than his counterpart. The American faces a 12-month tour, of which only half may be face to face with a corresponding Vietnamese. His counterpart, on the other hand, has almost invariably known a long series of advisors, and the present incumbent represents just one more eager face in a passing parade. Against this setting, the American must pursue a process which consists of successively discerning, appraising, communicating, and hopefully overseeing implementation. More often than not it entails frequent reversals, repetition, and revamping toward ever more limited goals. He has nothing to enforce his suggestions except the remote and frequently unpalatable threat of withholding American resources. This advisory process was described by General J. F. Collins, former CINCUSPAC as "like trying to push—not pull—a string of wet spaghetti across a table."

Actuation of this imprecise process must take place in an environment almost totally foreign in both physical aspects and cultural outlook. Research analysts say that the major obstacles to the advisor's adjustment are not the obvious ones of language, food, and living conditions; but rather the varying cultural patterns that are encountered. In Vietnam as elsewhere in the Orient, the ancient concept of "face" offers one such pattern. Motivating the family and unit-oriented Vietnamese toward national goals is another especially challenging assignment for the advisor. Essentially, there is a conflict between the traditional American action-oriented philosophy and the deliberate, stoic attitude of the Oriental.

Obviously, the building of an effective relationship under these conditions is a function of the complex interactions of personality and intellect. The myriad of tips, hints, and pointers that have been amassed by the armed services attest to the multiple shadings that evolve. Most of these sources, however, do concur in a few universal guidelines for neophyte advisors.

Fundamental among these is that the objective in counterpart relationships is to build a degree of mutual respect through good leadership practices and simple courtesy. A happy discovery to most is that generally the international brotherhood of arms then responds to the same soldierly qualities the world over. Incident to any advisory tour, however, is an initiation period of watching, learning, and producing, before "acceptance" is realized. Ideally, this deliberate beginning culminates in a relationship of mutual confidence, fellowship, and understanding that still does not transcend a healthy objectivity on the part of the advisor.

Of paramount importance to the building of this camaraderie, regardless of the personalities involved, is a dedication to becoming part of the unit. This entails the decidedly unrevolutionary trait of persistence; persistence not only in the fleeting trials of combat, but also in the face of adverse living conditions, the monotony of inactivity, and the frustrations of frequently rejected advice.

Another somewhat incongruous trait for the military man is the restraint required to stand aside and permit the counterpart to accept the credit for a mutual success. Of this, Marine Lieutenant General Victor H. Krulak says: "If he is not the sort who can defer to the Vietnamese, willingly have him take the praise and credit, if he does not have the personality which will permit him to lead by suasion and not authority, if he does not understand these things, then he should not be an advisor."

The successful advisor must be technically competent, knowledgeable in area and language, and possessed of communicative and interpersonal skills. Of the advisors queried by the writer, 71 per cent cite "professional competence" as a "most desirable trait," and among a score of personality qualities mentioned—"adaptability," "sense of humor," "tact"—82 per cent indicated "patience" or the related, "understanding."

Interestingly, these qualities, aside from "patience" and "understanding" differ little from those traditionally identified with the successful leader. Douglas Southall Freeman's renowned maxim "know your stuff" becomes perhaps even more applicable, because as one advisor wrote in allusion to the advisor's solitary posture: "If you didn't bring the knowledge with you, it isn't there."

Physical courage is a universally admired quality that has earned immediate recognition through the ages. The challenge of combat to man's character has perhaps always been the overriding concern to the young advisor approaching his duties, as indeed it has been to the raw soldier marching to the sounds of the guns throughout history. Of this instinct, longtime advisor Colonel Bryce Denno, U.S. Army, cautions: "Few advisors in a war of counterinsurgency, regardless of their rank or duty, need seek opportunities to display their courage. Danger is everywhere; in the city as well as in the countryside, in higher headquarters as in the platoon."

The personality traits sought in the advisor are a bit more complex and interrelated with the aforementioned cross-cultural distinctions. The consensus on the need for patience reflects the basic conflict between the energetic Westerner and the unhurried Oriental. It is also rooted in the unfamiliar—at least to Americans—quasi-war quality of insurgencies. The experienced counterinsurgent does not consider war a suspension of normal life as we do, but perhaps the only way of life he has known. Hence, he girds for the long pull and seeks those few semblances of "normal living" that he can still enjoy. The resultant somewhat apathetic outlook on what Americans consider a life or death struggle is a fundamental barrier in the advisor-counterpart relationship. Indeed, this is the essence of the Communist challenge in "wars of national liberation." It was in this vein that the late Bernard Fall told the writer: "The American take-charge attitude is our own greatest enemy."

The ideal advisor, then, possesses all the normal military virtues in a high degree. Moreover, he has a capability to shift emotional gears across the range from objective appraisal and subtle communication to inspirational action, while keeping the objective in ever-sharp perspective.

The future of the advisor in Vietnam. The immediate and most challenging development is the reorientation of the ARVN toward Revolutionary Development. This revised mission means an increase in Vietnamese "clear and hold" type operations while U.S. and some Vietnamese units continue to search out and destroy the major enemy elements, which show no signs of abandoning the war of maneuver. A static security posture in the overwhelmingly rural areas will bring social, political, and economic factors into play where military considerations alone once dominated. It will also mean that the operational advisor who transitioned before from peace to war to liaison will now rechannel his efforts toward nonmilitary matters.

This evolution spotlights the sector and subsector advisors who first arrived in the spring of 1964. An analysis of their mission will illustrate the new objectives that now affect all advisors to some degree. Described as "the executors of the U.S. effort at its most productive end," the subsector advisor is charged with the military tasks of training and operational supervision of the local Popular Force units plus liaison with transient U.S. or ARVN forces. He has the civilian-slanted responsibilities of monitoring the activities of the USIS, and the ARVN Revolutionary Development Cadres.

Whatever the degree of progress in these efforts, it is evident that Vietnam will see closer associations between the Armed Forces and people than ever before with all the inherent hazards. This undertaking will entail not only a revision in mission, but also in attitude, which will ultimately revolve more surely than ever on the collective advisor-counterpart relationships at the lowest levels. General Lewis Walt says of the pacification-oriented advisors: "All efforts will start and stop under their influence." There are grave doubts expressed about the future of this new endeavor. Hanson W. Baldwin, Military Editor of the *New York Times*, sums it up succinctly: "I am not at all sure they [the ARVN] can be trained to perform these duties, but I am sure that we must make the attempt."

Although there is no current plan for Marine subsector and sector advisors in the Army pattern, a new facet has opened that introduces Marines into the Revolutionary Development picture. In 1966, ten officers were loaned to the AID for training and utilization as provincial advisors, and this year 20 more were added as advisors to Revolutionary Development Cadres. This necessitates their stepping out of uniform and devoting their attention to guiding the economic aid programs at the user level.

The prospects of this new project are intriguing. The results, which remain to be evaluated, may give an insight into the ability of the future advisor to transition from a purely military to an economic sphere. This concept could well find important application in postwar Vietnam, as well as in the early stages of future insurgencies.

A final topic which might be considered a natural evolution of the advisor role is in the integration of U.S. and Vietnamese units. This is a working and successful reality in the III Marine Amphibious Force's Combined Action Company concept. This meshing of a Marine squad with three squads of popular forces into platoons and then companies has been strongly endorsed by two Marine Commandants. Baldwin considers this "the most helpful way of using South Vietnamese manpower . . . yet attempted and represents a logical extension of the duties of the advisor to the new phases of the war." This technique for providing local security uses an American as company commander, assisted by a Vietnamese Executive Officer, and imposes on the Commander as well as the integral squad leaders many of the ramifications of advising. Although he has the important advantage of operational command, he still must communicate and motivate successfully in the same type of environment that surrounds the advisor.

This is far from a new innovation. Smedley D. Butler was but one of a succession of legendary Marine figures—Sgt. Lewis B. "Chesty" Puller was another—who trained and led the various Gendarmeries of the "Banana Wars." More recently and more pertinently, battalions that were half-French Union and half-Vietnamese fought long after native units had disintegrated at Dien Bien Phu.

Far from being eclipsed, the American advisor will be in the forefront of both the "war of movement" against the main enemy forces and the continuing war for the hearts and minds of the people. He will transition progressively, as enemy strength ebbs, to a role perhaps best approximated by the new venture into the AID realm. He may conceivably become more involved in integrated efforts with consequent increased authority. Unquestionably, he will be called upon, as he has been for the 13 previous years, to adapt abruptly and unerringly to new trends and dynamic situations. Equally predictably, the measure of his success will be the measure of confidence he is able to inspire in his diminutive counterpart, whose stakes in this test tube war remain the highest.

The future of the advisory concept in any insurgency environment. The foregoing examination of the counterinsurgency proving ground that is Vietnam has traced the gamut of advisory activities as they have unfolded against the panorama of insurgency situations. The experiment is far from completed. We can accurately forecast the direction of some advisory efforts and others are pure speculation. The Communist enemy in Vietnam continues to follow Mao's strategic blueprint to the letter. The only speculation can be the degree to which he will pursue the Phase III warfare that he calls the "strategic offensive," or whether he will be compelled through diminution of resources or political expediency to revert to Phase II or even Phase I.

While the final analysis in Vietnam must be postponed, our experiences to date provide a basis for pondering the future. Such efforts are spurred by chilling reminders from all quarters that we can indeed expect to be challenged by new Communist-inspired insurgencies in the future. Vo Nguyen Giap has said: "South Vietnam is the model of the national liberation movement of our time. . . . If the special warfare that the U.S. imperialists are testing . . . is overcome, then it can be defeated anywhere in the world."

It is painfully obvious that we cannot maintain sufficient forces throughout the world to smother every smoldering insurgency, even if our presence was everywhere politically acceptable. The advisory structure provides us with the flexibility to maintain a "front line" representation around the world, which is at once symbolic, contributory, and relatively inexpensive. If properly employed and staffed to meet the pattern of aggression, the introduction of operational forces might be precluded altogether, or at least reduced in its proportions.

The decision to commit a MAAG of Vietnam proportions in a preventive capacity would of course depend on an accurate appraisal of the subversive threat by either the host nation or country team members already on the scene. Ideally, we would detect and immediately blanket an insurgency in its Phase I festering. An optimum sequence of introduction of MAAG elements, consistent, of course, with the receptiveness of the host nation, would occur simultaneously at the lowest possible level—battalion, training center, and district or comparable political subdivision. All observers concur that advisory effectiveness increases dramatically as representatives reach lower echelons. Colonel Bevan G. Cass, U.S. Marine Corps, an extraordinarily successful attaché in the 1965 Dominican crisis, even states unequivocally that "the only effective advising is at the lowest levels." The necessary balance between advisors and the supporting establishment is a limiting factor in the size of a MAAG, especially in politically sensitive countries. As an ex-advisor put it: "Parkinson's Law is a real threat." However, an expensive logistical tail can be curbed coincidentally with a gain in rapport by a determined advisory effort to integrate as completely as practicable into the native establishment.

A contingent of well-trained, carefully selected advisors working jointly and in an unhurried atmosphere, toward nation-building and increased effectiveness of the armed forces, could return with interest the initial cost of injecting such a MAAG structure. The specific direction and slant of their efforts would be determined, as it has been through history, by the dynamics of the particular situation; however, certain tenets should apply. For example, the mix of advisory talents, military and civilian, should be tailored to the peculiar requirements of the situation, and back-up tiers should respond accordingly. As one war correspondent wryly put it: "If they wanted helicopters and a heavy allotment of Baptist preachers and could document their demand in terms of their locale and its problem, those things would go into the team . . ." An accent on engineering-type skills and special talents in the political and sociological fields will probably be of increased importance in the makeup of future advisory elements.

A second major guideline would be continual emphasis on the closest possible assimilation into all aspects of host country life. This would only perpetuate the long-time policy of Marine Corps advisors in Vietnam who have habitually subsisted with their counterparts rather than in the various MACV compounds. This collective identification with the host nation should be enhanced by a degree of fluency in the native language and a length of tour that contributes to the continuity of the working relationship. This would offset Bernard Fall's criticism that "even the best advisor can't accomplish much in six months." The association fostered by these measures would perhaps more closely approach that of the Peace Corps than the traditional MAAGs.

Should the insurgency then flame into the active guerrilla warfare associated with Phase II, advisors who had trained their military units in counterinsurgency would accompany them into combat and evaluate their preparation in the field. Simultaneously, the necessary counterinsurgency measures could be applied in the nonmilitary areas, according to preconceived procedures. Additionally this broad advisory base should provide an intelligence-gathering capability that could detect insurgency trends and reduce our response time accordingly.

If all these measures failed to halt a further deterioration into a war of movement, the advisor could effectively abet the build-up of second and third-tier back-up forces. Also, indigenous forces should be pre-oriented toward specific roles in relation to U.S. operational forces. Conceivably, the predominantly security role newly assigned the ARVN today would be appropriate, or perhaps there would be needed a degree of integration such as represented in our Combined Action Companies. Possibly, even reconnaissance in the tradition of American Indian Scouts would be most useful. Whatever the eventuality, it should be preplanned, and the locally oriented. Intelligence-conscious advisor is the key to its implementation.

Advisory team members could well be the nucleus for an operational staff arriving on the scene, actually assuming assignments for which the groundwork had been previously laid. However, they would logically serve best as they serve today—in a liaison role where their rapport permits them to speak with the authority of the indigenous commander, thereby reducing the inevitable frictions generated by the intervention of foreign troops. Indeed, the advisory mission's own demeanor should well establish the atmosphere of acceptance into which operational units could come. Should the command of indigenous or integrated units become a reality, the advisor who has earned his home team "letter" is the obvious choice.

In keeping with the credo of "first in, last out," the advisory sequence should perform equally in reverse. The successful containment of Phase III should prompt the earliest feasible withdrawal of operational units, with the MAAG returning to its original configuration. If the insurgency is totally suppressed, or political considerations dictate, the advisory structure should be systematically withdrawn. The support and intermediate-level echelons should depart first, leaving the sector and subsector advisors or their equivalents until last. At this stage these advisors might well exchange uniforms for civilian clothes and proceed in the pattern of our AID advisor today. In fact, they might well become a stay-behind element in the Peace Corps pattern. This is not unprecedented in our history. In 1901, soldiers in the Philippines were given the option of returning home for demobilization or remaining as teachers. Some did stay, and many prominent Filipinos, including former Ambassador Carlos Romulo, were products of soldier-taught schools.

Should the presence of a complete MAAG structure be politically unfeasible; even a handful of advisors, provided they could be inserted at the lower levels, would provide a symbolic American presence. Secondment (temporary assignment) to the foreign service, in the British tradition, would offer one more possibility of achieving the same representation. For this, too, there is an American precedent in the seconding of Marine and naval officers to the Dominican government's Gendarmerie during the "intervention era."

Whatever course the advisory role of the future takes, it is safe to assume that heavy reliance will rest, as it always has, on the abilities of the individual advisor. The most unwieldy system can be made to work, and can be ultimately refined by able officers, while the closest adherence to the soundest of systems will falter with inadequate personnel. Obviously, priority of selection and appropriate training of advisors can pay incalculable dividends in money saved and, more importantly, in lives, both our own and those of friendly nations.

Along with these broad professional talents required of future advisors are the personality traits that will always shape the counterpart relationships that spell success or failure in any program. Their critical importance has been aptly demonstrated in Vietnam, and they will not change in the future world that awaits us. Our current selection processes should be adequate to provide the blend of knowledge, maturity, confidence, and adaptability we seek.

Looking ahead, then, it is evident that the advisory concept will continue to play a vital counterinsurgency role in its current configuration. However, it may hold an even greater potential for service in the preventive capacities that reduce or remove the causes for insurgency. This will mean a trend toward duties that are progressively more nonmilitary. As our national efforts to improve human circumstances increase, our worldwide representation will grow but will become increasingly more decentralized. Obviously it is in the best interests of our service and country that the Marine Corps keep pace and ensure a substantial participation in this representation. The broad talents sought in these individuals are but a projection of the self-reliance so traditionally revered in the Marine small unit leader. The record of nearly two centuries of expeditionary service have given present-day Marines a legacy of decentralized, many-sided incursions on foreign shores. The advisory crusades of tomorrow represent a logical extension of this tradition that could become the brightest chapter yet in an enduring record of difficult tasks well done.

A graduate of the U.S. Naval Academy with the Class of 1953, **Lieutenant Colonel Leftwich** has served in the Second Marine Division as a platoon commander (1954 to 1955), a company commander

(1960 to 1962), and as Aide to the Commanding General (1962 to 1963). His overseas duty includes Okinawa and Japan (1955 to 1966) and Advisor to the Vietnamese Marine Corps, Vietnam (1965). He has been a company officer at the Naval Academy (1957 to 1960), Aide to the Commandant, Marine Corps Schools (1963 to 1964), a Tactics instructor at Quantico (1966), and a Systems Analyst at HQMC (1967 to 1968). He is now Marine Corps Assistant/Aide to the Under Secretary of the Navy, Washington, D.C.

12 "Tribute: Colonel John Walter Ripley, U.S. Marine Corps (Retired)"

John Grider Miller

U.S. Naval Institute *Proceedings*
(December 2008): 27

EARLY ON EASTER SUNDAY 1972, Marine Captain John Ripley was certain that he was a dead man. By that day's end at Dong Ha, when his children—twelve time zones behind—were beginning to rummage through their Easter baskets, he figured he would be lying face down in the mud. Never again would he see his peaceful home in Virginia's Blue Ridge Mountains, a world away in more respects than one.

But when Ripley looked around and saw young Vietnamese Marines ready to face death with him, his mindset toughened and a sense of calm—familiar to warriors through the centuries—began to take hold. As he recalled later, "When you know you're not going to make it, a wonderful thing happens. You stop being cluttered by the feeling that you're going to save your butt." Thus unencumbered, he could face the day and focus on the task ahead.

It was a formidable task, that of destroying a Seabee-built steel-and-concrete highway bridge, capable of supporting 60-ton tanks. This had to be done before the vanguard of a North Vietnamese infantry and armor invasion force could cross.

117

Ripley was up to the job. After excelling in Naval Academy tests of applied strength and agility, he had proceeded to hone his physical conditioning and experience hands-on demolitions training with such elite units as Marine Force Reconnaissance, the Army's Rangers, and Great Britain's Royal Marines. Of all the captains in the Marine Corps at that time, few—if any—could match Ripley's qualifications. And circumstances had placed him barely a mile from the bridge, with time running out. Deprived of food and sleep for three days, John Ripley was running on adrenaline. But he was ready to give it a go.

The rest is history—and the stuff of legend. By destroying the bridge in time, Ripley stalled a North Vietnamese offensive and gave the South Vietnamese defenders time to regroup along the My Chanh River—a line they held. Saigon got a three-year reprieve and John Ripley received the Navy Cross.

By the time of his death at 69 last month in Annapolis, Colonel John Ripley had been memorialized by a diorama at the entrance to the Naval Academy's Memorial Hall and by Ripley Hall at the Academy's preparatory school in Newport. He also was an early selectee—and the first Marine so honored—to the Distinguished Graduate hall of fame established by the Naval Academy Alumni Association. The National Museum of the Marine Corps stands in silent tribute to his years of planning and fundraising on its behalf.

Perhaps John Ripley's greatest legacy can be found in his years of principled leadership, before and after 1972. He has been—and will continue to be—an inspiration to Marines of all ranks, as well as midshipmen and other would-be Marines. His full schedule of public appearances continued through the final week of his life, despite persistent and severe health problems.

His basic message, both as a teacher and as a prep school and university president, never varied:

One person can make a difference.
You are never beaten until you quit.

John Ripley lived by those words. As one of his sons said, "Once my dad set his mind to doing something, he would not quit; once he got the bit in his teeth, there was no stopping him." Yet his hard-driving approach to life did not keep him from fully enjoying his family and his wide circle of friends across the country and around the world.

As the epitome of courage in trying times, John Walter Ripley will remain an inspiration to a great and growing number of people far into the future. He is truly a man for the ages.

John Miller, a retired Marine colonel, is the author of *The Bridge at Dong Ha* (Naval Institute Press, 1989) and *The CoVans: U.S. Marine Advisors in Vietnam* (Naval Institute Press, 2000). Following his 1985 retirement from the Marine Corps, he became Managing Editor of *Proceedings* and *Naval History*, a post he held until 2000.

13 "Fury from the Sea: Marines in Grenada"

Lieutenant Colonel Michael J. Byron, USMC

U.S. Naval Institute *Proceedings*
(May 1984): 119–31

NOTE: *In the wake of considerable unrest last October on the Caribbean island of Grenada, the United States was called upon to restore peace and order and to rescue U.S. citizens whose safety was threatened. The resulting military operation was appropriately named—Urgent Fury. The urgency was needed not only because of the threat to American lives but also because of the possibility of Soviet-Cuban subversion. The fury came in the form of a joint task force, involving all U.S. military services. Key roles were played by the Navy–Marine Corps team, and the usefulness of amphibious warfare capability was once again demonstrated.*

ON THE MORNING of 25 October 1983, elements of Joint Task Force 120 conducted simultaneous amphibious and airborne assaults on the Caribbean island of Grenada. Their mission was to protect U.S. citizens and other foreign nationals and to restore peace and public order to the island. The reason for the operation, code-named Urgent Fury, was the rapid and almost total disintegration of governmental institutions and public order in Grenada following the 19 October murder of Prime Minister Maurice Bishop and other government and civilian leaders.

The likelihood was high of a continued, violent internal power struggle which would endanger U.S. and other foreign nationals on the island. Major forces for the operation came from all U.S. military services, supplemented by contingents from six Caribbean states. Despite unexpected Cuban and Grenadian resistance, in three days, these combined forces attained all key mission objectives on the island and evacuated a total of 599 American citizens and 80 foreign nationals.[1] Subsequently, the U.S. forces were instrumental in helping the Grenadians reestablish viable and representative governmental institutions.

Forces participating in operation Urgent Fury were specifically instructed to minimize casualties and property damage. U.S. casualties totaled 18 killed in action and 116 wounded. Of the Grenadian dead, 24 were civilians, including 21 killed in the accidental bombing of a mental hospital adjacent to an active antiaircraft site. The joint task force found 784 Cubans on the island; of these, 25 were killed in action and 59 wounded. The remainder were evacuated to Cuba.[2]

The combined forces found detailed evidence of Soviet and Cuban intent to subvert sovereign governments in the Caribbean to further communist objectives. A large quantity of Soviet-supplied weapons was captured on Grenada. These weapons would have eventually provided a military capability totally disproportionate to the needs of Grenada's population of 110,000. With this evidence, one could readily conclude that Grenada was destined to become another way station, in the "revolution without frontiers," for the export of subversion into the northern tier of South America and Eastern Caribbean States. The irony in operation Urgent Fury is that an action intended as a preventative measure had a curative effect.

In many respects, Urgent Fury was unique. The conflict proved a paradigm of limited military actions, particularly in the Third World environment. It featured a "come as you are" scenario typified by critical, time-sensitive mission requirements; minimal planning; employment of joint and combined forces; incomplete intelligence; command, control, and communications intensity; and high political visibility. These critical elements were balanced by several advantages. Among them: The relative proximity of Grenada to the United States; the lack of enemy opposition during deployment; the unsophisticated nature of enemy opposition; access to facilities in Barbados; and availability of a major, established U.S. operational facility at Roosevelt Roads, Puerto Rico. This combination of factors is unlikely to reoccur in future conflict scenarios.

Although Urgent Fury was a strategic and tactical success, we must exercise caution in determining the relevant lessons from the operation. However, one major lesson has been consistently visible from the outset: the absolute utility of the mobility and tactical flexibility inherent in naval amphibious forces during the campaign. To place their participation into a perspective for analysis, one must start with some background on the area.

The Grenadian Setting

Grenada, the "Isle of Spice," is a tourist's dream come true—120 square miles of mountainous terrain and rugged coast, lush tropical vegetation, one of the most picturesque ports in the Caribbean, and sunny beautiful beaches. The alluring image depicted in travel brochures fades quickly when compared with the realities and challenges imposed by the military geography of the island. The participants in operation Urgent Fury encountered a far different Grenada.

The island is the southern terminus of the Antilles Archipelago that extends 2,500 miles from Florida to Venezuela, separating the Atlantic Ocean from the Caribbean. Grenada is the southernmost of the Windward Islands, a subgrouping of the Antilles chain named because they are exposed to the northwest tradewinds. This translates to irregular, high surf on the exposed windward side of the island—a challenge that would be encountered and overcome by the amphibious task force on D-Day.

Grenada is approximately 86 nautical miles from the northeast coast of Venezuela and 58 nautical miles southwest of St. Vincent, its nearest neighbor in the Windwards. The relative proximity of Grenada to the United States—approximately 1,750 miles from Fort Bragg, North Carolina—greatly facilitated the deployment of airborne/air-landed forces during the operation. The island, which is oval in shape, is approximately 20.5 miles in length and 11.8 miles at its greatest width. Its area of 133 square miles is roughly twice the size of the District of Columbia. Grenada includes as dependencies the southernmost Grenadine Islands, an arc of small islands extending from Grenada north to St. Vincent. Carriacou, the largest, has an area of only 13.5 square miles.

Grenada, like the other Antilles, is volcanic in origin. The predominant topographic feature is the ridge of mountains which extends down the entire length of the island. This central cordillera, partially severed in several locations by steeply sloped valleys, extends almost through the entire width of the island as well. The steeper slopes are found on the west of the island and the more gradual on the east and southwest. The island's interior is formidable and characterized by escarpments, ravines, stream cuts, and the like. The coast is rugged, and suitable amphibious landing areas, drop zones, and helicopter landing zones are at a premium. Good cover from flat trajectory fire is available throughout the island. Grenada is edged by a discontinuous coastal plain. From St. George's south and east around the island to Grenville, the coastal plain is broadest, in some places up to 10 kilometers wide.

Grenada has a tropical climate with an average annual temperature of 82°. The rainy season runs from June through December with the wettest month being November. Forces participating in operation Urgent Fury, which was conducted in late October, were affected by rain squalls. Prevailing winds are from the east-northeast. On the windward side of the island, irregular plunging surf of one meter or higher can be encountered year-round.

Vegetation on the island is typical of a tropical climate and ranges from dense undergrowth on the coastal plain to double canopy jungle in the Grand Etang rain forest in the interior. In the majority of areas, the dense foliage restricts ground maneuver and off-road movement of tactical vehicles. At minimum, it affords excellent concealment from ground or aerial observation.

The terrain throughout St. George's parish is characterized by highlands that channelize movement and provide excellent fields of fire. This is generally apparent along the main avenue of approach from Point Salines to the city of St. George's. It is specifically evident in areas where the highlands come close to the seacoast and within the city limits of St. George's itself. As subsequent events would show, effective use of terrain by a determined defender can rapidly reduce a battle to the simplest of equations—infantryman against infantryman. These facts provide a basic geographic frame of reference, but Grenada's location must also be viewed from a strategic perspective.

Grenada is located athwart a key transit zone for strategic materials and oil. In time of war, unfriendly access to facilities on the island would jeopardize the flow of shipping. In conditions short of war, Grenada's strategic value lies in its geographic proximity to the northern tier of South America—Colombia, Venezuela, Guyana, Suriname, French Guiana, and Brazil, as well as to the rest of the Eastern Caribbean States. Grenada's potential as a transit point and support base for the export of revolution into the northern tier made the island most attractive to the Soviets and their Cuban surrogates.

The causes of Grenadian instability were deeply rooted. Grenada, in common with most of the micro-states in the Antilles, had perennial socioeconomic problems that were exacerbated in the late 1970s by the worldwide inflationary spiral that drove up the prices of virtually all necessary imports, particularly petroleum. Grenada suffered from overpopulation and underemployment. Moreover, the Grenadian population is concentrated in the coastal areas with 30% of the population located in St. George's alone. The economy is principally based on the export of agricultural products which are extremely susceptible to international market fluctuation. The cultivation of tourism as an alternative met with mixed results. This industry was depressed as well, and austere Grenadian facilities could not compete within the limited market.

The eccentric Sir Eric Gairy, who was obsessed with witchcraft, astral projection, and unidentified flying objects, dominated the Grenadian political scene for years and, by late 1979, had lost almost all popular support due to his penchant for self-aggrandizement and the use of brutality to intimidate the populace. Gairy had created paramilitary squads (one of which was called the "Mongoose Gang") to further cement his power. These measures failed to stifle the growth of left-wing opposition groups on the island.

Grenada's drift into the Cuban/Soviet sphere of influence began in March 1979, when Maurice Bishop, leader of the leftist New Joint Endeavor for Welfare, Education and Liberation (JEWEL) Movement took advantage of Prime Minister Gairy's temporary absence and staged a near-bloodless coup. In a radio address to the nation the day of the coup, Bishop assured the people of Grenada that all democratic freedoms, including the freedom of elections, religion, and public opinion would be fully restored. The new People's Revolutionary Government combined the populist nationalism of Bishop and the Marxism of Deputy Prime Minister Bernard Coard.

Cuban Premier Fidel Castro moved quickly to solidify ties with the new government and to offer military and economic assistance. By late 1979, Grenada had received small-arms shipments from Havana, and it became evident that Maurice Bishop had no intention of fulfilling his promise of early and free elections. Suspending the island's constitution and speaking against traditional parliamentary democracy, Bishop announced that a new revolutionary course, based on the Cuban model, would be charted for Grenada. By early 1980, Grenada's transition to a Marxist state appeared irrevocably set in motion.

Grenada's position as a close ally of the Soviet Union and Cuba appeared solid until an intra-party feud came to a head in October 1983. Bishop's power was openly challenged by the ultra-leftist Coard. The rift had been developing for some months and focused on a party decision, orchestrated by Coard, to limit Bishop's one-man rule by establishing a council form of government, with Coard as chief policymaker. Coard was clearly dissatisfied with Bishop's slowness in converting Grenada into a truly socialist state. Bishop apparently refused to go along with Coard's grab for power, and after a heated discussion at a 12 October party meeting, Coard resigned his post as Deputy Prime Minister and quickly began rallying his supporters for a showdown with Bishop. The following day, Bishop was arrested. Coard had apparently secured the support of the majority of the New JEWEL Movement and the Army, commanded by General Hudson Austin. The liberation of Bishop from house arrest by his supporters, the subsequent march on Fort Rupert (named after Bishop's father, who was killed by Gairy's police during street demonstrations in 1978), the shootings there that took the lives of Bishop, several cabinet ministers, and scores of others, and the imposition of martial law and formation of a revolutionary military council to govern the island were the key events that pointed to a continued, violent internal power struggle on the "Isle of Spice."

The Protagonists

In January of 1981, the Bishop government restructured its armed forces under the umbrella organization of the People's Revolutionary Armed Forces (PRAF). The PRAF was composed of the standing People's Revolutionary Army (PRA), the People's Revolutionary Militia (PRM), the Grenada Police Service (GPS), the Coast Guard, the Prison and Fire Services, and the Cadet Corps. General Austin, a former prison guard, assumed command of both the PRAF and PRA. By 25 October 1983, the PRAF had a regular army of 600, supplemented by a militia estimated to be between 2,500 and 2,800.[3]

Almost 900 Cuban, Soviet, North Korean, Libyan, East German, and Bulgarian personnel (including permanent military advisors) were found on the island. Of the 900 man total, 784 were Cubans. Fifty-three Cubans were identified as military advisors on the PRA staff, in field units, or in security-related positions. Six hundred thirty-six fell in the category of "construction worker." Cuba has had a comprehensive and strictly enforced compulsory military service law since August 1963. The most recent version of the law (1973) mandates active or reserve military service for at least three years with the military obligation continuing until age 50.[4] Given the high level of Cuban military activity throughout the world as well as the requirement for compulsory military service, a substantial level of military expertise on the part of the Cuban "construction" workers must be assumed. This has been further substantiated by evidence of Cuban control of resistance to the multinational force on Grenada and reports of Cuban participation in combat.

The weaponry of the People's Revolutionary Armed Forces included state-of-the-art Soviet-supplied infantry weapons, as well as 12 ZU-23 antiaircraft guns, eight 73-mm. SPG-9 recoilless guns, and BTR 60 armored personnel carriers. The role the ZU-23 antiaircraft guns would play in the ensuing battle is particularly noteworthy. First fielded in the early 1960s, the ZU-23 is a prime example of a system which, when properly emplaced to capitalize on terrain and channelized approaches and employed by well-trained crews, can provide utilitarian service far in excess of its projected technological life span. The Grenadan ZU-23 crews were among of the most highly trained members of the People's Revolutionary Army. Weapons were well situated for point defense of key areas in St. George's as well as the Salines and Pearls airfields. Captured range cards indicated that the crews had been well briefed on the operating characteristics of U.S. aircraft.

The threat posed by armed factions on Grenada to U.S. nationals, particularly the 600-plus medical students at the St. George's University school of medicine heightened in light of the increased probability of a violent internal power struggle. The United States began to determine the availability of forces should the need arise.

Joint Task Force 120 was activated on 23 October 1983 and the Commander, Second Fleet, Vice Admiral Joseph Metcalf III, was named commander. The naval amphibious forces (Task Force 124, commanded by Captain Carl R. Erie) selected by U.S. Commander in Chief Atlantic for operation Urgent Fury consisted of Amphibious Squadron Four, which included the USS *Guam* (LPH-9), USS *Trenton* (LPD-14), USS *Fort Snelling* (LSD-30), USS *Manitowoc* (LST-1180), and USS *Barnstable County* (LST-1197) with the 22nd Marine Amphibious Unit (Colonel James P. Faulkner) embarked. The Marine amphibious unit comprised Battalion Landing Team 2/8 (Lieutenant Colonel Ray L. Smith), Marine Medium Helicopter Squadron 261 (Lieutenant Colonel Granville R. Amos), and MAU Service Support Group 22 (Major Albert E. Shively), along with a small MAU headquarters element.[5] The 22nd MAU, like all Marine air-ground task forces, is a task-organized, combined-arms force including an integral supporting air combat element.

On 18 October, Amphibious Squadron Four, with embarked Marines, sailed for the Mediterranean where they were scheduled to relieve the U.S. contingent in the multinational force in Lebanon. They would participate in a NATO exercise in Spain en route. Prior to departure, intensive training had been conducted in amphibious operations, night helicopter assaults, and noncombatant evacuation. Many of the Marines were veterans of previous tours in Lebanon. More than 40% of the battalion's personnel had been with the unit two years or more.[6]

The Operation

The murder of Maurice Bishop and the establishment of a 24-hour, shoot-on-sight curfew on Wednesday, 19 October proved to be the catalyst for the commencement of contingency planning in Washington. Although the gradual internal breakdown of governmental institutions on the island had been monitored closely since Bishop's house arrest on the 13th, serious planning for noncombatant evacuation operations had not yet begun.[7] The potential for a violent internal power struggle in the wake of Bishop's death and the increasing danger to the more than 600 U.S. medical students prompted the activation of the National Security Council crisis management mechanisms.[8] During the evening of 19 October, a Joint Chiefs of Staff warning order for the conduct of noncombatant evacuation operations was sent to CinCLant.[9] Courses of action were requested. Early on the morning of 20 October, the National Security Council interagency Crisis Pre-Planning Group met to consider the situation in Grenada. It decided the situation was serious enough to warrant immediate consideration by the National Security Council's Special Situation Group, chaired by Vice President George Bush. During the day, assessments were refined and options were prepared for the Commander in Chief. As a preliminary precaution, the USS *Independence* (CV-62) battle group and Amphibious Squadron Four with the embarked 22nd Marine Amphibious Unit—already en route for the eastern Mediterranean—were directed to change course and steer closer to Grenada on their transit across the Atlantic.[10]

Following the recommendations of the special situation group, President Reagan directed that noncombatant evacuation planning continue. Paralleling U.S. concern, the heads of state of the Organization of Eastern Caribbean States (OECS) plus nonmembers Jamaica and Barbados met in Bridgetown, Barbados, on Friday, 21 October, to discuss the recent events in Grenada. The Eastern Caribbean countries determined by unanimous vote that conditions in Grenada (a fellow OECS member) required action under the 1981 treaty to protect the region. The OECS asked Barbados, Jamaica, and the United States to assist them. The initial OECS request, received in Washington on 21 October, noted the current conditions of anarchy and the threat to peace and security in the region created by the lack of authority in Grenada. It requested the United States join them in a military operation to restore order and democracy. This request for help required further deliberation by the special situation group, since a military operation would, under these circumstances, extend beyond the limits of noncombatant evacuation. A revised action plan to support the Organization of Eastern Caribbean States request was prepared for the President. After extensive deliberation, he approved the operation, in conjunction with OECS participants, to restore democratic government on Grenada.

It should be noted that throughout this entire planning process, operational security was paramount. Washington principals were directed to maintain regular scheduled activities. However, all remained in constant touch with the situation throughout the planning phase. Late on 22 October, in response to Presidential direction, the Joint Chiefs of Staff provided the Commander in Chief Atlantic, Admiral Wesley McDonald, with confirmation of the expanded mission. Operation Urgent Fury was to be conducted not later than dawn 25 October. CinCLant had little more than 48 hours to assemble his forces, plan, and execute the operation.

Early Sunday, 23 October, the tragic news of the suicide bombing of the Marine battalion landing team headquarters in Beirut, Lebanon, reached Washington. The President returned from Augusta, Georgia, and convened a meeting of the National Security Planning Group to assess the situation.[11] The issue of the bombing's impact upon the impending operation on Grenada was raised. In spite of the political risk of the operation, the President affirmed that he had an obligation to U.S. citizens in danger and to the Caribbean nations that had requested assistance. He issued a final confirmation of the decision to move ahead with the operation.[12] On the 23rd, the first U.S. Atlantic Command liaison officers arrived aboard the *Guam* and commenced detailed coordination with operational elements.[13] They were followed on the 24th of October by Commander Joint Task Force 120, Vice Admiral Metcalf, and his staff.

From the perspective of the amphibious forces, arrival of liaison personnel late on 23 October provided the first details on the expanded mission and scope of Urgent Fury 2nd necessitated a major adjustment in planning. Initial Planning had focused on only a unilateral Navy–Marine Corps effort in the Salines-St. George's area. The island was now to be divided into two separate operating areas. The boundary would roughly divide the island in half and follow the general trace of the road between St. George's and Grenville. Objectives in St. George's were assigned to U.S. Army forces. Landings in both north and south were to occur simultaneously.

Planning continued throughout the amphibious forces on 24 October. The revised plan assigned, among other things, responsibility to the commander of the amphibious task force for the northern area and the mission of seizing Pearls airfield and other key terrain and the protection of U.S. and designated foreign nationals. The preliminary plan was to conduct a heliborne assault on the Pearls Airfield-Grenville complex followed, at H + 30, by a surface assault of forces who would subsequently assist in the expansion of a lodgement area.

At approximately 2200, D–1 (24 October), Navy SEALs were inserted in the northern beaches, in spite of adverse weather conditions, in the vicinity of Pearls to conduct a beach reconnaissance. By 0300 on D-Day, reports had been received from the SEALs indicating that beach conditions were marginal for amphibian assault vehicles and unsuited for landing craft.[14] Reporting was delayed somewhat until the SEALs successfully ex-filtrated from amongst the People's Revolutionary Army security personnel guarding the airfield. The SEALs were not detected.

In the few hours remaining until H-hour, the commander of the amphibious task force and the commander of the landing force quickly shifted to the alternate landing plan. Company G, 2/8, was embarked on the USS Manitowoc (LST-1180). This unit was scheduled to conduct the surface assault and subsequently assist in expansion of the beachhead. The men of Company G were directed to remain embarked until conditions improved. The landing zone for Company E, originally tasked to land by helicopter directly on Pearls Airfield, was moved 700 meters to the south when intelligence was received on active People's Revolutionary Army antiaircraft sites on the hill to the north of the airfield. Company F remained scheduled to conduct a helo assault into landing zone

Oriole near Grenville and subsequently to secure the city and key road junctions. Initial assault waves went off on schedule for a 0500 H-hour, but a combination of darkness and ground fog delayed first touchdown until 0520. The lead aircraft carrying Company E into the new landing zone south of the airstrip drew enemy antiaircraft fire. The company suffered no battle casualties. The antiaircraft sites were engaged and subsequently neutralized by the Marine amphibious unit's AH-1T Cobra gunships. The shift of the landing zone, in response to intelligence, had disrupted planned People's Revolutionary Army defensive fires and had landed the Marines in an area at the far limits of effective range of the PRA 12.7-mm. antiaircraft guns. The airfield complex was quickly secured. Two 12.7-mm. antiaircraft guns and a number of small arms were captured. A Cuban AN-26 aircraft and a 12-man aircrew which had delivered a Cuban colonel the day before were captured. The colonel was to organize the defense of the island, but he was too late. He subsequently availed himself of diplomatic sanctuary.

Company F, 2/8, was inserted, without opposition, and by 0630 commenced movement into Grenville. Later that morning, a single amphibian assault vehicle would land over the Pearls beach in an attempt to determine the feasibility of a surface landing. Through a combination of skill and good luck, the vehicle made it ashore, but the preliminary assessment of the SEALs was confirmed. The beach conditions were not suitable for use. Company G and the remaining 13 of 14 assault vehicles would remain on board the *Manitowoc*. Within several hours, this would prove fortuitous for the entire joint task force.

Concomitant with the initial D-Day activities of Joint Task Force 124, a U.S. Army ranger task force conducted airdrop/airland operations to seize the Salines airfield complex. The landing was later than planned and came under fire. Resistance, which was heavy, initially came from several antiaircraft weapons situated overlooking the airfield and, subsequently, from Cuban and Grenadan forces athwart the main avenue of approach from Salines to St. George's.[15] In spite of the opposition, the airhead was gradually expanded.

Initial Caribbean Peacekeeping Forces commenced their closure into Salines and, by 1400 that afternoon, the first two battalions of the U.S. 82nd Airborne Division began to land. Enemy fire in the vicinity of the airhead continued after the initial assault. Moreover, it became increasingly clear that some of the Cuban "construction" workers were as adept with their AK-47 rifles as they were with shovels. Manifestations of overall Cuban command of the defensive effort became evident.

At 1200 at D-Day, Commander Joint Task Force 120, Vice Admiral Metcalf, actively began to consider additional tactical options for bringing the conflict to a prompt and decisive conclusion without needless loss of lives or collateral property damage. Marine Corps air support in the form of AH-IT Cobra gunships was diverted into the Army sector to provide air support to the U.S. elements in the Governor General's residence. People's Revolutionary Army forces, utilizing armored personnel carriers, had counterattacked and had pinned the personnel in the residence. Antiaircraft sites were active within the city of St. George's and from the commanding high ground overlooking the residential areas. The Cobras engaged PRA antiaircraft sites, but in the course of the ensuing action two aircraft were shot down resulting in the deaths of three Marine pilots and the wounding of another.

In the face of continuing enemy resistance, Admiral Metcalf made the decision, by early afternoon D-Day, to land the Marines into the Army sector in the vicinity of St. George's. This move would reassign some of the Army objectives to the Marines. A boundary change was effected to accommodate the arrival of the Marines.

The tactical plan for Pearls and the northern zone was quickly adjusted. Company F was directed at 1400 to return to landing zone Oriole to prepare for a helicopter assault into the vicinity of St. George's. E Company, the battalion landing team's 81-mm. mortar platoon and the 2/8 Bravo command group consolidated defensive positions overlooking the Pearls airfield, commenced aggressive local patrolling, and established an evacuation control center that would eventually transfer 47 evacuees to the USS *Trenton* (LPD-14). Locals began to provide invaluable information on the location of People's Revolutionary Army members and weapons caches.

The circumstances that left Company G embarked on board the *Manitowoc* were now to pay off. The LST got under way immediately with the rest of the amphibious task force (except for the *Trenton*), following in trace around the southern coast of Grenada. By 2000 on D-Day, Company G, reinforced by amphibian assault vehicles and tanks, was ashore at Grand Mai and the amphibious forces had completed their second assault of the day under combat conditions. The story of the selection of Grand Mai as a landing site was, strangely enough, paralleled by a Royal Marines experience during the 1982 Falklands campaign. They were able to draw extensively during planning upon the personal knowledge and experience of Major Ewen Southby-Tailyour, who had commanded the Royal Marine Detachment in the Falklands. An amateur sailor, Major Southby-Tailyour had travelled throughout the islands by small boat and had even published a navigation guide for private circulation. Fortunately for the U.S. amphibious task force, the chief staff officer of the squadron, Commander Richard Butler, another small boat aficionado, had visited Grenada several years prior while on vacation. He recalled the hydrography of the Grand Mai area and recommended it as a landing site, thereby filling an important intelligence gap at a critical juncture in the operation.

Preparations continued that night for the assault into St. George's. Company F assembled at landing zone Oriole, Grenville and conducted a cross-island night helicopter-borne assault. They were inserted at 0300, D + 1 into helicopter landing zone Fuel, which was adjacent to the Grand Mai beachhead.

Company G was given the mission of securing the Governor General's residence. At 0400 D + 1, Company G conducted a night attack and by 0700 had rescued 33 personnel including the Governor General, Sir Paul Scoon. Numerous weapons, to include recoilless rifles, 23-mm. and .50-caliber machine guns were captured en route. Company F, reinforced by tanks, Dragon, and TOW elements and the battalion landing team reconnaissance platoon, attacked south and occupied the Queens Park Race Course. At 1100, Company F moved onto the Gretna Green highground. Company G then continued the attack to secure Fort Fredrick. This was accomplished by 1700. Concomitantly, the reconnaissance platoon occupied Fort George.

In the southern zone, the airborne task force which had assumed operational control of the Rangers late on D-Day, consolidated at Point Salines airfield. Operations were commenced in the Mome Rouse area. Continued opposition was encountered.

At midday on D + 1, Admiral Metcalf directed a joint Marine/Ranger Battalion heliborne assault on the Grand Anse campus of the St. George's University School of Medicine where additional American students were discovered to be. The assault was conducted at 1600 that afternoon. Two hundred twenty-four U.S. students were rescued and returned to Point Salines. One Marine CH-46 helicopter was lost due to enemy action. There were no casualties.

Ground operations continued on the island on Thursday, 27 October, which was D + 2. U.S. Army elements from Task Force 121 attacked the police academy at Grand Anse and moved into the Ruth Howard area. A vertical assault, using U.S. Army helicopters, was conducted on Calivigny Barracks. Marines continued the attack to secure key terrain in St. George's. The Richmond Hill Prison, Fort Adolphus, and Fort Lucas were secured by Company G by 1000. E Company, moving out from Pearls airfield, secured the Mt. Home Agricultural Station at 1422 and captured large quantities of People's Revolutionary Army arms.

H Battery, 3rd Battalion, 10th Marines, was landed at Grand Mai as a provisional rifle company and moved to Queens Park Race Course. H Battery assumed security for the battalion landing team command group and prisoner of war camp. Company F then moved south into St. George's proper and secured the Botanical Gardens, Belmont, and the Ross Point Hotel.

D + 3, 28 October was a day for consolidation. U.S. Army elements swept through the Lance aux Epines peninsula and evacuated another 202 U.S. medical students. A linkup with Marine Corps elements at Ross Point Hotel was effected. Marines consolidated positions in St. George's and Pearls and commenced identification and screening of People's Revolutionary Army members. Marines recovered documentation which revealed the existence of five secret military agreements between the PRA and the Soviet Union (three), North Korea, and Cuba.

On D + 4, Marines maintained static strong point positions and continued to assist in the restoration of government services and control in St. George's. Army elements conducted a reconnaissance in force through Richmond Hill, Mt. Hartman, and the Egemont Peninsula. Caribbean Peacekeeping Force elements arrived in the Pearls area and began coordination for the relief of Company E, 2/8. Bernard and Phylis Coard, Leon James, and Selwyn Mrachan—key actors in the overthrow and murder of Maurice Bishop—were captured by Marines from H Battery.

At 0330 on D + 5, a 90-man patrol from E Company, 2/8, left the Pearls airfield in a motorized movement to secure Sauteurs. The company moved by jeep and commandered civilian vehicles. No resistance was encountered. Equipment and a People's Revolutionary Army battalion commander were captured. Sauteurs was secured by 0915. Company F was relieved by Caribbean Peacekeeping Force personnel and moved to Queens Park Race Course in preparation for future operations. Company G, 2/8, with amphibian assault vehicles moved north at 1500 in an aggressive reconnaissance in force to liberate Gouyave and Victoria. They were supported by Cobra gunships, Navy close air support, naval gunfire, and followed up the coast by an LCU with tanks. Only scattered small arms fire was encountered. Army elements continued to sweep the southeastern peninsula and prepare to replace Marine forces throughout the island.

By 1500 on D + 6, 31 October, Battalion Landing Team 2/8 backloaded aboard respective vessels after relief in place by elements of the

Caribbean Peacekeeping Force and 82nd Airborne Division. The remaining tasks on Grenada were turned over to the Army and amphibious forces got immediately under way for Carriacou Island.

The island of Carriacou lies north of Grenada. Intelligence identified People's Revolutionary Army units and arms caches on the island. Simultaneous helicopter-borne and surface assaults were conducted at 0530, 1 November. Surprise was complete and no resistance was encountered. Company F captured a large cache of weapons at Belair House. By 1400, all PRA had surrendered or were captured. Later that day, Company G backloaded aboard the *Manitowoc*.

On 2 November, F Company and the Battalion Landing Team Alfa command group were relieved in place by elements of the 82nd Airborne Division. Backload was rapidly completed and the amphibious ready group and embarked Marines were under way for Beirut.

The Lessons

Operation Urgent Fury was a strategic and tactical success. Mission objectives were achieved with minimal casualties. The ability of U.S. forces to plan and execute a complex operation in an extremely compressed time period was demonstrated.

This type of operation may well be a precursor of conflict in the Third World in the coming years. Without a doubt, the "come as you are" nature of the operation, with rapid fusion of joint and combined forces, minimal planning data to include intelligence and high political visibility, will be seen again by U.S. planners.

The conduct of Urgent Fury was facilitated by favorable logistic, geographic, and operational variables. These fortuitous elements are unlikely to appear in future conflict scenarios.

From the naval perspective, the Grenada experience served more to highlight old lessons and to validate training and operational philosophy rather than to identify new requirements. Salient among these lessons are: first, the continued utility of amphibious forces in regional crisis response. Second, requirement for tactical flexibility to accommodate the Clausewitzian "fog and friction" of a come-as-you-are crisis.

The strategic mobility of amphibious forces made them quickly available for participation in operation Urgent Fury. In the post–World War II period, four out of five of the more than 215 incidents requiring use of military power to achieve national objectives involved naval forces. True to this pattern, the first forces to move in Urgent Fury were naval.

The ready availability of amphibious forces provided the national command authority with more options for use in crisis resolution ranging from psychological suasion to a forcible entry capability. Had the need for military force on Grenada failed to materialize in Grenada, naval forces would have continued into scheduled deployments without sending premature or inappropriate signals. The precautionary movement of ground forces, particularly during a period of crisis assessment, poses an infinitely greater risk. The narrow constraints on the mode of their deployment and relative inflexibility during insertion tend to convert any significant deployment into a clear national commitment.

The departure of amphibious forces from the United States on 18 October for a NATO exercise and subsequent relief of the U.S. contingent of the multinational force in Lebanon, although routine, was highly publicized by the media. Under this smokescreen, the diversion of this force during transit across the Atlantic posed minimal operations security problems. In accordance with standard operating procedure, the amphibious task force was combat-loaded and ready for immediate employment.

The logistic advantage accrued to the joint task force commander by the use of self-deployable and self-sustaining forces must not be overlooked because of the proximity of the objective area to the United States, the availability of airlift, and the relatively low intensity of combat. In a different scenario, the sustainability provided by the war reserve stocks embarked on the amphibious task force would be a far more significant asset.

The Grenada experience again highlighted the utility of amphibious forces as a viable and flexible instrument of national policy. Amphibious forces provide a significant capability for controlled crisis response at a relatively small cost. However the current paucity of amphibious shipping limits the potential of this unique capability.

Rarely do operational plans provide all the solutions to the challenges of a combat situation. In virtually every conflict scenario, there are operational variables that cannot be quantified such as the weather, degree of enemy resistance, and the effect of terrain. These can only be overcome by tactical innovation and flexibility, applied within the framework of an operational philosophy that allows for the "friction and fog" of war. Such a philosophy has long been the hallmark of the Navy–Marine Corps team. Its enduring message was sounded again in clarion tones during Urgent Fury.

The immediate transition to an alternate landing plan at H-2 on D-Day, the rapid planning and execution of the Joint heliborne assault with Army Rangers into Grand Anse, and the aggressive reconnaissance in force operations throughout the northern area of operations are examples of tactical innovation and flexibility fostered by this Operational philosophy.

The best example occurred on D-Day.

With enemy resistance in the southern operational sector, Admiral Metcalf redirected the amphibious task force from operations in the northern region to relieve the pressure in the south. Marines readjusted the ground scheme of maneuver, amphibious ships moved quickly, and hasty plans were developed while en route. In less than four hours, combat units landed at St. George's, stunning the defenders with armored shock power. Marine tanks and amphibian assault vehicles struck quickly. This tactical coup de grace diverted pressure from the U.S. combat elements engaged in the south and broke the heart of People's Revolutionary Army resistance on the island. This also pointed up the value of combat power. The inherently greater firepower and mobility of the Marines psychologically undercut the Cubans and the PRA and made discretion on their part the better part of valor.

In the span of seven days, amphibious forces executed three amphibious combat assaults, all during the hours of darkness and under poor landing conditions. Each assault was, in turn, followed by a backload. All of these evolutions transpired under stringent time constraints. The amphibious task force not only provided command and control facilities, and logistic and medical support for its embarked forces but for those of Joint Task Force 120 as well. Finally, the amphibious warfare ships provided a vital safe haven for noncombatant evacuees.

As Clausewitz indicates, "In war, the will is directed at an animate object that reacts." The key element in combat is flexibility—the inherent ability to cope with challenges, both expected and unexpected. As long as this element is in demand, the amphibious mission will be as viable as ever.

Notes

1. U.S. Departments of Defense and State, *Grenada: A Preliminary Report* (Washington, D.C.: n.p., 16 December 1983), p. 1.
2. Ibid.
3. U.S., Departments of Defense and State, op-cit., p. 18.
4. U.S., Defense Intelligence Agency, *Handbook on the Cuban Armed Forces*, (Washington, D.C., n.p., 1979), p. 1–13.
5. Ronald Spector, "Marines in Grenada," top secret Marine Corps Historical Center, Washington, D.C., p. 2.
6. Ibid., p. 3.
7. Washington level crisis management has been described in various sources. One of the best ones is "Grenada: Anatomy of a 'Go' Decision," Ralph Kinney Bennett. *Reader's Digest*, February 1984, pp. 72–77.
8. See Les Janka's "The National Security Council and the Making of American Middle East Policy," *Armed Forces Journal International*, March 1984, pp. 8486, for a definitive account of the National Security Council's structure for policy formulation.
9. U.S., Department of Defense, "Question and Answer Session with Senior Defense Official," Saturday, 29 October 1983, TS, Acme Reporting Company, Washington, D.C., p. 2.
10. Ibid., p. 3.
11. Bennett, p. 75.
12. Ibid., p. 76.
13. Spector, p. 7.

14. Robert Bernal and Christopher Grey, "Grenada," *Marines*, January 1984, p. 8.
15. U.S., Department of Defense, "Question and Answer Session with Senior Defense Official," pp. 14–17.

Bibliography

Bennett, Ralph Kinney. "Grenada: Anatomy of a 'Go' Decision." *Reader's Digest*, February 1984, pp. 72–77.

Bernal, Robert, and Grey, Christopher. "Grenada." *Marines*, January 1984, pp. 7–10.

DeFrank, Thomas M., and Walcott, John. "The Invasion Countdown." *Newsweek*, 7 November 1983, p. 69.

Diederich, Bernard. "Images from an Unlikely War." *Time*, 1 November 1983, pp. 30–31.

Janka, Les. "The National Security Council and The Making of American Middle East Policy." *Armed Forces Journal International*, March 1984, pp. 84–86.

Kling, Bill. "Advance Warning Hindered U.S. Operations in Grenada." *Washington Times*, 9 November 1983, p. 1.

Magnuson, Ed. "D-Day in Grenada." *Time*, 7 November 1983, pp. 22–28.

Mullin, Dennis. "Why the Surprise Move in Grenada and What Next?" *U.S. News and World Report*, 7 November 1983, pp. 31–34.

Spector, Ronald. "Marines in Grenada," top secret, Marine Corps Historical Center, Washington, D.C.

Tift, Susan. "A Treasure Trove of Documents." *Time*, 14 November 1983, p. 30.

U.S. Defense Intelligence Agency, *Handbook on the Cuban Armed Forces*. Washington, D.C.: n.p., 1979.

U.S. Department of Defense. *Grenada: October 25 to November 2, 1983*. Washington, D.C.: n.p., 1983.

U.S. Department of Defense. Question and Answer Session with Senior Defense Official (SDO), Saturday, 29 October 1983, TS. Acme Reporting Company, Washington, D.C.

U.S. Departments of Defense and State. *Grenada: A Preliminary Report*. Washington, D C.: n.p., 16 December 1983.

Whitaker, Mark et al. "The Battle for Grenada." *Newsweek*, 1 November 1983. pp. 66, 68–69, 72, 75–76.

Lieutenant Colonel Michael J. Byron is an action officer in the western regional branch of the Plans Division, Plans, Policies and Operations Department, Headquarters, U.S. Marine Corps. He was graduated from the University of Miami (Florida) in 1963 with a B.A. degree in Latin American studies. Following his commissioning in 1963, Lieutenant Colonel Byron took Vietnamese language training. He served two tours as an advisor to the Vietnamese Marine Corps and one combat tour with the 1st Battalion, 3rd Marines, USMC. After duty with the 2nd Marine Division, he was assigned to the U.S. Military Mission in Greece and attended the Armed Forces Staff College and Interamerican Defense College. He has had duty in J-3, Joint Chiefs of Staff, was executive officer of the 4th and 9th Marines, 3rd Marine Division, and has been involved in the Norway prepositioning program.

14 "Rolling with the 2d Marine Division"

Lieutenant General William M. Keys, USMC

U.S. Naval Institute *Proceedings*
(November 1991): 77–80

NOTE: *General Keys, now the Commanding General, Fleet Marine Force Atlantic, was in command of the 2d Marine Division at Camp Lejeune, North Carolina, when Iraq invaded Kuwait in August 1990. By the following February, as it prepared to breach the Iraqi defense line, the 2d Division had become the heaviest division—packing the most combat power—in Marine Corps history.*

PROCEEDINGS: THE MARINE CORPS bases on the West Coast started emptying out almost immediately, once the balloon went up. What was going on at Camp Lejeune?

Keys: Everyone was tracking the situation, and some units were getting ready to go. Initially, all that mounted out was the 4th MEB [Marine Expeditionary Brigade], which was in process of leading out for Norway, to conduct an annual NATO exercise in the Teamwork series. After a little reconfiguring, they deployed to the Indian Ocean.

The ground combat element of the 4th MEB was the 2d Marine Regiment, which left me with two infantry regiments—the 6th Marines and 8th Marines. Since it was quite possibly headed for combat, we let the 4th MEB go out a lot heavier than we should have—particularly in the combat service support elements. I guess we figured that someday we'd link up out there, but I never saw the 2d Marines again, for the duration of Desert Shield and Desert Storm. In the meantime they were floating around with assets that the rest of us would need when the time arrived for us to mount out. There's a lesson in there somewhere.

Between August and December, we tried to track developments in Southwest Asia through situation reports and intelligence briefs. We received several warning orders that were later canceled: first, to send another regiment; next, to mount out another MEB, this one designated to marry up with gear carried into the theater of operations by an MPS [Maritime Prepositioning Ships] squadron. Late in November, we got the word that the entire 2d Marine Division would go over there and fight under command of I MEF [Marine Expeditionary Force], which in effect would become a corps-level command.

When we received the mount-out order, I still had the two active-duty regiments—the 6th Marines and the 8th Marines. The rest of the 2d Division was filled out with reserves, about 4,000 of them. We filled up our holes and added an extra Reserve tank battalion. We had a comprehensive individual training program for each reservist: rifle range, gas mask, Code of Conduct—the whole works. At the same time, we were giving the same training to the reservists who were destined to join the 1st Marine Division, already deployed to Southwest Asia. We put about 15,000 reservists through this program in roughly one month. Camp Lejeune looked like it must have looked during World War II, with Marines reporting at all hours of the day and night, finding temporary billeting in a tent or barracks, then starting out the first thing next morning to train for combat.

We began flying the 2d Division to Saudi Arabia around 12 December. The shipping for our heavy gear and supplies (one MPS squadron plus 18 break-bulk ships) had begun sailing around the last of November and continued through December. All our gear had arrived by the middle of January; all the troops were there by year's end.

Proceedings: Then you got some reinforcements in Saudi Arabia, didn't you?

Keys: We took operational control of a U.S. Army tank brigade—the "Tiger Brigade" [1st Brigade, 2nd Armored Division]. They came fully equipped with M-1 tanks and were a first-class outfit. They had been together as a unit for about two years, and had been through the National Training Center [the Army's stateside equivalent of the Marine Air-Ground Combat Center in the Mojave Desert]. Their commander and officers really knew their stuff.

We spent the first few days getting to know each other, getting briefed on each other's procedures. That was much less of a problem than you might think. We go to their schools; they go to our schools. A lot of our training and doctrine is the same. Before long, we were one tight division. Right at the beginning, I told the Tiger Brigade that they were my third regiment, and would be treated the same as the other two. This made a great difference to them and paid off greatly later. Those Army tankers now wear the 2d Marine Division patch on their right sleeves—to signify their service with the Marines in combat. At the time we assumed operational control, they were located about 80 miles away, in a relatively good training area. I saw no point in moving them closer, so they stayed there until the first week in January and conducted their own training exercises. We'd go down there to observe and to coordinate some things with them that I wanted to do.

Proceedings: When did you begin moving toward your eventual attack positions?

Keys: About 28 December, the first elements of the division moved north. I wanted to move units into the field as soon as they got their equipment, and get on with some serious training. We moved into a place called the Triangle area—which was in fact a triangle, lying between three hard-topped roads—about 50 miles north of Al Jubayl. Within two weeks, the entire division was up at the Triangle.

We built a training range that could handle all the weapons of a mechanized and armored assault force, and we developed a complex of obstacles for use in training for breaching operations. In addition to their other work, every unit went through a standard syllabus that took about five training days. About the middle of January, we moved northwest to the left of the 1st Marine Division, about 12 miles below the border with Kuwait. We stayed there about two weeks, and—as we did everywhere we stopped—we kept on training. This is where we had our first significant contact with Iraqi forces. Some of our light armored vehicles had a skirmish with Iraqi tanks along the border and killed five, as I recall.

Proceedings: What were the Iraqis doing at this time? Were they trying to run any probes, any reconnaissance missions?

Keys: They would come up to the border at night, and if they did anything beyond that, it didn't go very deep. It was the same with us. CentCom didn't want anybody in the I MEF sector launching combat-reconnaissance missions into Kuwait at this point. The concern was starting the ground war early.

Proceedings: What was your scheme of maneuver at this time?

Keys: Our plans changed as circumstances changed. About the first week of February, General [Walter E.] Boomer [Commanding General, I Marine Expeditionary Force] approved a plan that called for the 1st Marine Division to conduct the breaching operation. Then the 2d Division would pass through the 1st Division's lines and become the exploitation force. At the time, we were driven to the one-division breach concept of operations because we didn't seem to have enough heavy breaching equipment to support two divisions.

There were many, many problems associated with this plan. For one, it was difficult to get the two divisions together for training and rehearsing. When we finally did some passage-of-lines rehearsing, it did not go well. Since both divisions were heavily mechanized, we might have had a column of vehicles stretching back 30 miles, just getting lined up for the attack. I personally did not care for this plan, but would have supported it if we were driven to it by the lack of breaching equipment.

But by 7 or 8 February, some additional equipment from the Israelis and the U.S. Army had arrived. In addition, my Tiger Brigade had some built-in breaching capability, and knew how to use it—in fact, they gave us a lot of help in planning the entire assault. So I went to General Boomer and asked him to consider my alternative plan. He agreed, and I showed him what I wanted to do. It was rather radical. It called for moving the 2d Division another 80 miles to the northwest and breaching right through one of the Iraqi oil fields. The field we picked was supposedly one of the worst, because of heavy concentrations of hydrogen gas. But we had two or three Kuwaiti resistance fighters with us, and one—who had worked in that field—said that we could probably get through it. If things got too bad, we could always use our gas masks. They were not the most effective filtering devices for hydrogen, but they would do in a crunch.

As I presented this plan to General Boomer, I related my confidence in my subordinate unit commanders and the Marines and soldiers of the 2d Division and I guess it showed through—because he approved the plan (pending General Schwarzkopf's approval). This brought about a major change in the I MEF concept of operations.

Proceedings: It also brought about a major change in the logistical support concept, didn't it?

Keys: It sure did. Brigadier General [C. C.] Chuck Krulak [commanding the Direct Support Command] was there, and General Boomer asked him if he could support the new plan. Chuck said he could, but not from his current location. So in two weeks he carved out a massive logistical support area in the desert, where he was able to support both divisions. I just want to add this about General Krulak and his Direct Support Command. They were right up there with us the entire way, and we owe a large part of our success in the attack to Chuck Krulak as an individual and to the superb performers in his command.

Next, General [H. Norman] Schwarzkopf [Commanding General, the Central Command] came down. We briefed him and he said the plan sounded good. So we were cleared for action. As another aside, I think General Schwarzkopf was a superlative commander—a commander's commander. You could just tell that he knew what he was doing. He instilled a lot of confidence in his general officers. I have a lot of respect for the man as an individual, a soldier, and a commander.

Proceedings: What happened next?

Keys: I directed the 6th Marine Regiment to prepare to conduct the breach. We would do a one-regiment breach, with each battalion, in turn, cutting two lanes through the barrier. We moved the 6th Marines into a sterile area and started to construct an exact replica of the barrier line that we would have to breach. We gathered all the intelligence we could on the area. We sent people back to CentCom headquarters, and we even sent the Division Engineer back to the Defense Intelligence Agency in Washington, D.C., for anything they could find. From photos and imagery we developed a schematic map with a scale of 1:25,000.

The Division Engineers did a superb job of building a barrier to scale, in a short time. Then their commanding officer, Colonel Larry Livingston, Commanding Officer of the 6th Marines, took his units through, battalion by battalion. After one week of training, he reported that he was ready to go. I can't say enough about the way he put it all together.

Next, we moved everybody some 80 miles to the breach area. Our moves over there were mostly self-moves. I had an extra truck company attached to the division, and a total of 672 trucks at my disposal—and I needed every one of them. At times when I needed more, I could rely on our Force Service Support Group and even contracted civilian trucks—but as we got closer to the war, the civilian trucks got less dependable. My point is that—especially in the desert—you need trucks and logistical vehicles to accomplish your mission, and the only vehicles you can count on in every situation are the ones that actually belong to you.

Proceedings: Once you got near the breach site, how did you organize your forces for the attack?

Keys: I put the division in a laydown site, in the order they would go into the assault. The 6th Marines were right in front of the area to be breached. The second unit through would be the Tiger Brigade, followed by the 8th Marines. I sent the Army tank brigade second—to lead the exploitation forces—because they were totally equipped with night-vision devices. The Marines were limited in this regard, but every soldier had what he needed and every Army vehicle had what it needed, and it was the best gear on the market. They truly had an exceptional night-fighting capability, and it made a difference. My thinking was that if the initial penetration by the 6th Marines went slowly, and dragged into late afternoon or evening, the Tiger Brigade could move up and complete the breach during hours of darkness.

My overall aim was to push as much combat power as possible through those two breach lanes, as quickly as possible. Going into the assault, the 2d Marine Division had a strength of about 20,500, with 257 tanks, including 185 M-1s. It was probably the heaviest Marine division—with the most combat power—ever to take the field.

The assault was scheduled for 22 February. General Schwarzkopf asked if we'd be ready to go. I said, "Yes. I'd like to have more time, but I'll be ready to go into the assault then, if that's the date."

He said, "What I'm more concerned about is the weather."

We delayed the assault for two days, waiting for better weather. The weather just got worse. So we put our heads down and kicked off the assault on 24 February, even though the weather was still rotten. The night before, we had made 18 cuts in the berm line with artillery, so we were ready for a fast start. But the morning fog was so dense that we couldn't see 100 yards ahead. With visibility that bad, we couldn't count on much in the way of close air support—but we punched on through. Contrary to some reports, the Iraqis were still there, waiting for us. They fired about 300 rounds of artillery as we worked to breach the minefields, but they had no forward observers to coax the fire on target, so we could discount the prospect of heavy casualties from their shots in the dark. Aside from mines, Iraqi artillery had been my major concern, so I felt early on that we were off to a good start.

We punched on through the barrier, and by the evening of the first day all of the 6th Marines, the Tiger Brigade, and four battalions of artillery had moved through the breach. The following morning, I brought the 8th Marines through, and we prepared to continue the attack that afternoon with the Tiger Brigade on the left, the 6th Marines in the center, and the 8th Marines on the right. Light armored vehicles, which had entered Kuwait early (CentCom's policy had changed late in the game), performed scouting and reconnaissance missions on the left flank, while units from the division's reconnaissance battalion screened the right flank.

I need to digress again. The light armored vehicles, in their first combat test with the Marines, really proved their worth—shooting and moving, shooting and moving. They killed more Iraqi tanks than we realized at first, and they took the first Iraqi prisoners. An Iraqi general we captured on the second day told us that he misidentified the first infiltration of light armored vehicles as the main armored attack, even though we had planned it as more of a diversionary attack.

Intelligence sources told us that we would probably come into contact with the 80th Iraqi Tank Brigade, their operational reserve force, attacking into our center. But large-scale attacks never materialized, and we now think that the 80th Brigade was just folded back into the Iraqi 5th Mechanized Division, which both the 1st and 2d Marine Divisions eventually chopped to pieces.

We captured 5,000 Iraqi prisoners the first day. They would take us under fire. We would return fire with effect—killing a few—and then they would just quit. That proved to be the pattern for the entire 100-hour war. Once we took them under heavy fire, they'd fire a few more rounds, then quit.

On the morning of the third day, General Boomer cleared me to drive on Kuwait City, using the Tiger Brigade to envelop to the west, sealing off an area called Al Jahar. Around 1000 that morning, I called in my subordinate commanders to give them mission-type orders. I didn't give them much time to prepare, but they still managed to jump off around noontime. When we got within ten miles of Kuwait City, I cut the Tiger Brigade loose to envelop to the left. They sealed a major intersection on the escape route to Iraq, and trapped thousands of fleeing Iraqis. By the evening of the third day, we were poised to enter the city the next morning. In the morning, the word came down: "Don't go." The Coalition forces from the region had been selected to enter Kuwait City. The following evening, we met with them at Al Jahar, to coordinate the passage of lines. We held onto a line called the Six-Ring Road; they passed through our lines and entered the city. That was the plan all along.

Proceedings: What about the timing of the cease-fire?

Keys: I think it probably came at the right time. At least it seemed that way when the word came down. In retrospect, it is clear that we could have done a lot more damage to the Iraqi forces if we had pressed on more quickly. It now appears that they started bugging out of Kuwait as soon as we crossed the southern border. But at the time it would not have made sense to expose our forces to counterattacks by overextending ourselves, under the assumption that the enemy would never fight. That's how it looked at division level, anyway. Overall, I tend to agree with the President: If we had pursued the retreating forces into Iraq, we'd still be in Iraq now—and would probably be there for the next hundred years. We didn't manage to nail the major culprit in all of this, but we did what we had set out to do.

Proceedings: A few questions still linger, after the war. How effective was your intelligence support?

Keys: At the strategic level, it was fine. But we did not get enough tactical intelligence—front-line battle intelligence. The RPV [remotely piloted vehicle] worked very well, but we needed many more of them, plus systems to disseminate their information to all units that needed it. In my opinion, the RPV is going to be our best tactical intelligence-gathering vehicle in the future, and we need to develop that program.

Our electronic warfare assets—for example, the Radio Battalion—worked very well. We also received a lot of information from Marine aviation. They'd fly a mission, and when they got back they'd immediately call the division's combat operations center to report whatever they saw. That was close to real-time intelligence support.

I guess that our biggest overall intelligence shortcoming was in building Saddam Hussein and his forces into a monster that just wasn't there. Going into the battle, this made us more gunshy than we should have been. Certainly, the Iraqis had more equipment and capability than any force we've ever faced. But the fighting spirit just was not there. The individual foot soldiers were badly abused by their leaders—not necessarily their military leaders, but their government—and low morale was the result. I think their senior military leaders knew what they were doing. After we seized Kuwait City, we uncovered several sand tables depicting their defenses that were incredibly detailed. They were fully prepared for us. They had thousands of weapons and millions of rounds of small-arms and tank ammunition—so they could have put up one hell of a fight if they had wanted to. Their defensive areas were well organized, and had they chosen to put their hearts into it, we would have had a real fight on our hands.

I guess it all boils down to the fact that the individual Iraqi soldier did not measure up to, say, the North Vietnamese soldier. The Iraqis were not ready to die for what they believed in—whatever that was.

And that's it in a nutshell.

15 "An Entirely Different Battlefield"

Ed Darack

U.S. Naval Institute *Proceedings*
(November 2008): 36–40

MORE THAN JUST A LINE from the oldest official hymn in the armed forces of the United States, the words "In every clime and place" articulate one of the central pillars of the U.S. Marine Corps ethos: the readiness to deploy anywhere in the world in defense of the nation—in any and all environmental conditions. Success during deployment, of course, depends greatly on a given unit's training before embarking on a mission, training that practitioners unanimously agree should mimic the conditions of the upcoming area of operation in addition to honing basic warfighting skills.

For Iraq-bound units, that training cycle culminates in a one-month workup at the Marine Air Ground Combat Center (MCAGCC) at Twenty-nine Palms, California. There, under the watchful eye of personnel of the Tactical Training and Exercise Control Group (TTECG), deploying units endure the rigors of a harsh desert environment while undertaking simultaneous, live-fire combined arms exercises that bring together elements of the Marine Air Ground Task Force, or MAGTF—arguably the most potent means of kinetic warfighting, where an infantry unit maneuvers onto a target under the direct support of artillery, mortars, tanks, and rotary- and fixed-wing aircraft. The combat center also trains units for support roles as well as non-kinetic missions.

Every unit deploying to Iraq ultimately cherishes the lessons learned from training at the center, which has been known by various names. In its current iteration—Mojave Viper—infantry experience the heat of the midday sun inside an AAV7 amphibious assault vehicle while encased in often crushing body armor. Members of fire support teams, or FiSTs, experience the frenetic pace of working to guide their fire onto targets. The command elements immerse themselves in the details of an ever-evolving battlescape where they must ensure force protection, the balanced sustainment of troops, and support intelligence gathering and analysis efforts, all while maintaining solid communication and a strong backbone of command and control. After a Mojave Viper training evolution, Marine Corps units often find the desert of western Iraq, half a world away, less alien.

Train for the Environment

But what about those units bound for the heights of Afghanistan—or other mountainous corners of the globe in future conflicts? Full range, live-fire MAGTF training is absolutely essential for Marine Corps units deploying anywhere on the planet; but so is immersion in an environment specific to where a unit will travel. The Mountain Warfare Training Center, located at Pickel Meadow, near the town of Bridgeport in California's eastern Sierra Nevada, has proven vital for Marines deploying to Afghanistan over the course of Operation Enduring Freedom.

Established in the wake of the "Frozen Chosin" campaign of the Korean War in 1951, Bridgeport (as the base has come to be known) presents deploying Marines with the experiences of gasping for breath at high altitude, the cold of night and the biting chill of pre-dawn, and of course the knee-pounding and ankle-twisting movement across miles of steep terrain—just like Twentynine Palms immerses troops in the realities of desert living. But while the combat center provides a full-fledged MAGTF experience, Bridgeport has only a few ranges for sniper training, with no ability to host live-fire mortar, close-air support, and artillery training.

Captain Zach Rashman, a CH-53D pilot who served with the 2d Battalion of the 3d Marine Regiment as a forward air controller for the battalion's seven-month deployment to the mountainous provinces of eastern Afghanistan in 2005 described splitting training between live-fire at Twentynine Palms and the environmental experience at Bridgeport.

Had we done live-fire, full MAGTF training in the mountains, we would have been much better prepared. There were many, many factors and hurdles that combat in the mountains of Afghanistan presented us with that we would have been much better prepared to face had we done live-fire training in the mountains before deploying, and not had our training essentially broken between live-fire in the desert and non-live-fire in the mountains.

Many share Rashman's sentiments.

"We can't take complex terrain to Twentynine Palms, but we can bring full spectrum, live-fire, combined arms training to the mountains," stated Colonel Norman Cooling, who took command of the Mountain Warfare Training Center in July of 2008. Cooling commanded the 3d Battalion, 3d Marine Regiment in eastern Afghanistan from the fall of 2004 through the spring of 2005. While in the operating forces, he trained for and deployed to Afghanistan, then Iraq, in back-to-back succession.

Great Leap Forward

Today, Cooling and the staff at the Mountain Warfare Training Center seek to pioneer a quantum leap forward in mountain warfare training by establishing a live-fire and maneuver, combined-arms training complex—including the center's current training area coupled with existing and potential live-fire ranges in and around Hawthorne Weapons Depot in the high mountains to the south of Hawthorne. Cooling emphasizes that the envisioned mountain warfare training complex isn't intended to replicate training at Twentynine Palms, but complement it. He further qualifies the proposed training ground by explaining that while the mountains of the Combat Center represent positions from which a unit can dominate the surrounding desert plains, that luxury does not exist in the complex terrain at Bridgeport.

Cooling noted that the area, with elevations ranging from 6,000 feet up to more than 11,000 is very similar to the terrain of Afghanistan's Kunar Province. "The terrain dramatically changes the tactics, techniques, and procedures associated with the accomplishment of every military task." The terrain complicates everything from communication, to methods used to employ direct and indirect fires—from the M16 service rifle all the way up to aviation-delivered ordnance—to sustainment, and force protection. "It's an entirely different battlefield."

Artillery Considerations

Experts in the respective components of a MAGTF who have operated in Afghanistan enthusiastically agree with Cooling's position, including Captain Roe Lemons, currently of 1st Air Naval Gun Liaison Company and an artillery forward observer who served with the 2d Battalion, 3d Marines in Afghanistan during their 2005 deployment. "The idea of a full-scale, live-fire MAGTF training ground, dedicated to the mountains is a great and necessary idea. In the mountains, you really have to worry about trajectory," Lemons said. "Most gun lines [batteries of heavy artillery] sit in valleys in Afghanistan—very steep walled valleys. A target only a few miles away is often separated by a high, steep ridge, so you really have to elevate the gun, to shoot high angle, to lob the round over the high ridge. In the desert, you typically don't have to worry about that." Lemons also explained difficulties posed to forward observers. "In flat desert, you have a forward observer perched on key terrain, and he can get a strong feel for distances throughout the entire battlespace from that one spot. In the mountains, sometimes you're lucky to be able to see a mile. It can really throw you off."

The artillery officer then explained another factor crucial to mountain artillery work—elevation correction. In the desert, the gun line and target are usually at or near the same elevation, where in the mountains the difference could be 5,000 feet or more. This requires a complex ballistic solution that demands training. "It isn't something that you should face for the first time when lives are on the line in country." Mortars also present their own challenges in mountain battlespaces. Infantry officer Captain Patrick Kinser, the officer in charge of the Mountain Warfare Training Center's Formal Schools, described the challenges he faced with mortar fire in Afghanistan: "The greatest hurdle came from sustainment—in a desert environment like Iraq, you can move gun tubes around and re-supply a team by convoy. Not so in steep mountains like those of Afghanistan."

> In Afghanistan, you carry everything on your back, or if you are lucky, you can hire some donkeys to help out. But you have to absolutely be prepared to man-pack the tubes, the base plates, the bipods, the sights, and of course, the rounds, in backpacks. You never can leave the wire without mortars organic to your unit—even as small as a squad.

Air-to-Ground Difficulties

Mountainous terrain presents extremely challenging hurdles to aviators as well. "From a fixed-wing aircraft's position, the toughest problem in the mountains is target acquisition," stated Major Doug Glover, an F/A-18D weapon system operator who served as a forward air controller in Afghanistan from December 2001 through February 2002 for the 26th Marine Expeditionary Unit. "Even though we live in a world with GPS weapons, you still have to find the target, work to positively identify the target, and with complex terrain—moving fast in a jet—that can be a real challenge." Glover also noted the ramifications of altitude and effective threat proximity:

> If you are used to flying at 20,000 feet, with targets at or near sea level—and now your target is at 10,000 feet, then you are 10,000

feet above the ground; that much closer to a possible ground-to-air threat. So the solution to that is to fly at 30,000 feet—where your airplane flies very differently than at 20,000 feet.

Captain Rashman described some of the challenges he faced on the ground in Afghanistan that if practiced in a full MAGTF training environment—in the mountains—would produce far more thoroughly prepared units for an Afghan deployment. "Both the altitude and the terrain are so critical, for both troops and equipment. You can't expect a unit to be able to operate anywhere near full capacity at up to altitudes of 8,000 to 10,000 feet and beyond if they've trained at only sea level to 3,000."

The aviator then explained the effects on helicopters: "The higher you go, the thinner the air, meaning the greater the power required to keep the aircraft in the air. But also, because of the thin air, you have less power available. As a helicopter operator, you get squeezed between the two converging margins."

Rashman also explained how mountains foster turbulence, particularly while flying close to the ground, "orographic [mountain induced] turbulence can be very problematic—strong wind shear can come at you from all different, unpredictable, directions, sometimes pushing you toward the ground." As a helicopter aviator and someone who has served a rigorous tour on the ground in eastern Afghanistan as a forward air controller, he has seen both sides.

While controlling the air environment for numerous combat operations, the aviator quickly understood how steep, mountainous terrain posed challenges vastly different from other situations. Radio operators and forward air controllers must walk the mountains with a tremendous amount of gear. Backups are needed for everything, including the large PRC-117 radio. "We carried extra batteries, extra headsets, and 60mm mortar rounds to mark targets for aircraft." And there is the sustainment gear, weapons, body armor, and helmet.

Rashman explained some of the technical difficulties:

Communication is vital—you need to maintain comms at all times, and in the mountains, where you're rarely in line of sight of whom you want to talk to, you really have to know how to use non-line-of-sight frequencies and channels, like SATCOM. To be able to work out techniques before setting foot in a theater of operation—talking to air, infantry, commanders in the rear, in a live-fire training setting—would give troops a tremendous advantage.

Any Marine who has worked comms of any type in the mountains will attest to the often frustrating difficulties the terrain poses.

And It's Physical

Rashman and others who have worked in Afghanistan unanimously agree that mountainous environments can throw a variety of often-unforeseen physical challenges at troops. "Most people who've not operated in the mountains underestimate the amount of dehydration one experiences at altitude," said Staff Sergeant Keith Eggers, the staff noncommissioned officer in charge of Bridgeport's Mountain Leaders Course and a scout/sniper team leader who deployed to Afghanistan in 2005. He added that people often incorrectly consider all mountainous environments to be cold. "During the summer months in the Kunar Province, it regularly topped 110 and 115, even as high as 8,000 feet." And it's not just extreme heat in the summer and extreme cold in the winter. Eggers explained that mountains "create their own weather," and experience wide daily temperature swings:

It can be bone dry and hot one minute, then later in the day, a thunderstorm can appear out of nowhere over a steep ridge, dump icy rain, and then the troops will be shivering through the night. Combine this with the stress of combat, and it weighs on troops like no other experience. To replicate this before heading to theater is vital.

Lieutenant Colonel Robert Scott, currently the Commandant of the Marine Corps Fellow to the Center for Strategic and International Studies and former executive officer of 2d Battalion, 3d Marines during their Afghan deployment, summarizes the big picture of such a proposed training facility:

> It will challenge units to start thinking and working across longer distances and ensure that the staff is working the warfare functions across those distances. Afghanistan is an immature theater when compared to Iraq and the staff needs to learn the difficulties in working in an immature theater across those long distances. That would be the beauty of training in such a full-scale MAGTF mountain training ground.

Although not all of Afghanistan is comprised of complex mountainous terrain, Lieutenant Colonel Chip Bierman, who commanded the 1st Battalion, 3d Marines there in 2006, asserted "any Marine battalion deploying to Afghanistan must prepare for the possibility that it may end up operating in the mountains. . . . I think deploying with any other view is a mistake."

Tough on Everything

Getting the training ground up and running won't prove easy. "I agree 100 percent that we need a full spectrum, live-fire, MAGTF training ground in the mountains," stated Brigadier General Charles Gurganus, the commanding general of Marine Air Ground Combat Center, under which the Mountain Warfare Training Center is a subordinate command. "But to do this will require a huge commitment of personnel—expert personnel, essentially standing up another Tactical Training and Exercise Control Group specific to a mountain MAGTF training center. But it can be done."

Because of the joint nature of current and future military operations—to include those in mountainous environments—the Mountain Warfare Training Center staff hosts a number of units from other services and countries throughout each year. The proposed complex will of course continue this trend to bring in units of other services both to train and to support training, to develop the most realistic, relevant, up-to-date training experience.

Currently, the proposed site lies unused and virtually unseen. With a renewed focus on Afghanistan, and clear need for a real-world training ground for future threats in mountainous regions throughout the globe, however, this may soon change. Lieutenant Colonel Scott summarized the necessity best:

> To build combat effective units, the Marine Corps always takes a building block approach to training. . . . A Marine can fire expertly on a target, and a Marine can withstand shivering cold. However, can a unit get a Marine into position to fire expertly on a target *while* shivering cold and then follow up with non-kinetic operations? You have to create that experience.

Mr. Darack is an independent photographer and writer who covers a broad range of topics. His forthcoming book, *Victory Point* (Berkley Hardcover, 2009), recounts operations Red Wings and Whalers, which took place in Afghanistan's mountainous Kunar Province in the summer of 2005.

16

"The Meditations of a Lion"

Lieutenant Commander Thomas J. Cutler, USN (Ret.)

U.S. Naval Institute *Proceedings*
(January 2012): 92

Be a man of principle. Keep your word. Live with integrity. Be brave. Believe in something bigger than yourself. . . . Teach. Mentor. Give something back to society. Be a good friend. Be humble and be self-confident. . . . Appreciate your friends and family. Become the greatest husband and father ever.

READING THESE WORDS without attribution, one might reasonably guess they were the writings of Marcus Aurelius, the Roman emperor whose "Meditations" are included in any worthwhile collection of the great works of Western Civilization. But these are actually the words of a man of humbler—if no less noble—origin. Douglas Zembiec was a major in the U.S Marine Corps.

Like the emperor, he kept notebooks filled with thoughts that reflected his ambition to live a meaningful life. Among those many recorded aphorisms we should not be surprised to find such maxims as "Serve your country" and "Fight for what you believe in." Such aspirations are common among those in service to their country. And ideas such as "Lead from the front," and "Conquer your fears" are typical of young officers.

But it was on the battlefield Douglas Zembiec proved that he could wield the proverbial sword as well as the pen, that his notebooks were not mere philosophical musings, but a personal doctrine that guided his actions when faced with life-and-death decisions. With combat tours in Kosovo, Afghanistan, and Iraq, Zembiec became a respected leader of Marines.

But in 2004, while leading an assault in the Jolan district of Fallujah, then-Captain Zembiec cemented his reputation by standing on top of a tank to direct fire while insurgents rained rocket-propelled grenades and small-arms fire down from surrounding rooftops. Like Aurelius—who is known to history as one of "the good emperors" and was admiringly called "Philosopher King" by his contemporaries—Douglas Zembiec's actions in Iraq earned him a title of his own, bestowed by those who had seen him in action. Zembiec became known as the "Lion of Fallujah," a name derived from an interview in which he described—not himself— his men as having "fought like lions." He also told reporters that "ten million insurgents won't even begin to fill the boots of one of my men" and "there is no greater honor than to lead men into combat."

And Zembiec continued to lead men in combat. But on his fourth tour in Iraq, while leading a force of Iraqis he had helped train, the lion was felled by small-arms fire in a Baghdad alley.

A 1995 U.S. Naval Academy graduate, his funeral service was conducted in the chapel, the same one where he had attended Mass as a midshipman and where he had wed his wife, Pamela, just two years before. A constellation of stars glittered in the pews as at least 15 generals came to pay their respects. But Zembiec would likely have been more impressed by others who had also come to pay tribute to a fallen warrior—many of his "lions" came, some from great distances. One, Sergeant Major William Skiles, who had served as Zembiec's first sergeant, said "There is no one better to go to war with." As one officer in attendance later commented, "your men have to follow your orders; they don't have to go to your funeral." Aurelius, who had written "men exist for the sake of one another," would have smiled.

Lieutenant Commander Cutler is the author of several Naval Institute Press books, including *A Sailor's History of the U.S. Navy* and *Brown Water, Black Berets*.

INDEX

advisors and advisory efforts: achievements of advisory system in Vietnam,
105; Continental Army reorganization and, 98; counseling functions,
100–101, 102–3, 104; country teams,
99; courage and, 107–8; duties and
functions of, 99; early advisory
relationship, 98–99; evaluation of,
105; future of advisors in Vietnam,
108–10; future of advisory concept,
110–15; guerrilla attacks, combat
operations, and advisory functions,
101–3; liaison and coordination-
of-operations functions of advisors, 99, 103–5, 113–14; Military
Assistance and Advisory Group
(MAAG), 99, 100–101, 111–13,
114; Military Assistance Program,
99; relationship-building and traits
of advisors, 106–7; selection and
training of advisors, 105–8, 114–15;
skills of advisors, 101–2, 114–15;
stay-behind element, 114; technical instruction functions, 99, 104;
Vietnam War advisory efforts, 99,
100–115

Afghanistan: air-to-ground difficulties,
157–59; altitude challenges and
training for, 158; artillery sustainment and re-supply in, 157; artillery
trajectory and elevation correction
in, 156–57; physical challenges of
operations in, 159–60; training for
deployment to, 154–61
Air Force, U.S.: Korean War operations, 52, 53, 80–81. *See also* Army/
Army Air Forces, U.S.
aircraft, mountainous environments
and air-to-ground difficulties, 157–59
Alaska, 11
Almond, Edward M., 55, 62, 69
Amos, Granville R., 128
amphibious operations: amphibious
landings, 2; development of techniques for, 58; Grenada/Urgent
Fury operation, 120, 122, 131–34,
137–40; Inchon landing, 63–67,
81–82, 87; Korean War amphibious
operations, planning and preparations for, 53–63; utility of mobility
and tactical flexibility of, 87–88,
122, 137–40; World War II operations, 53, 54, 58, 67

training of for, 53; Observatory Hill Operations, 65; Pohang-Andong operations, 85–86; Pusan, importance of holding, 54; Pusan Perimeter, defense of, 55, 61; Red Beach landing, 61, 64–65; rice paddy patrols, 86; Ripper, Operation, 86; Seoul, capture of by North Korea, 52; Seoul operations, 67–70, 72, 85, 87; Sinhung-ni pass operations, 75, 76–77, 79–80; skill and discipline of CCF troops, 77–78; snow and operations during, 94, 95, 96; start of, 51–52; supplies and rations for, 75, 80–81, 82–83; supply operations at Red Beach, 65, 66; Taegu operations, 54, 55, 61; Task Force Drysdale operations, 78–79; UN forces operations, 53, 54, 55; U.S. forces for, 52–53, 59; weather during, 61, 64, 79–80, 89, 94, 95, 96; Wonsan landing, 71, 72–73; Yudam-ni operations, 75–76, 79–81, 82, 93
Krulak, C. C. "Chuck," 147
Krulak, Victor H., 107
Kuwait City, drive and entrance to, 150–51

Lebanon, 128, 130, 137, 138
Leckie, Robert, 34
Lee, 4
Lee, Willis A., 39
Lejeune, John A., 1, 2, 26
Lemons, Roe, 156–57
Lend-Lease plan, 40
Lion of Fallujah, 163
Litzenberg, Homer L., 69–70
Livingstone, Larry, 148
Low, Frederick, F., 11
Lucas, L. C., 20
luck, 27, 30
Lynch, 4
Lyon, H. W., 20

MacArthur, Douglas, 52, 53–54, 55–56, 62, 63, 64, 75

Machine Gun Battalion, 6th, 25–26
Magill, L. J., 20
Manitowoc, 128, 131, 132, 134, 137
Mansfield, 62
Mao Tse-tung, 100
Marblehead, 17–18, 20, 21
Marine Air Ground Combat Center (MCAGCC), Twenty-nine Palms, 144, 153–56
Marine Air Ground Task Force (MAGTE), 153
Marine Aircraft Group 33 (MAG 33), 53, 55, 68
Marine Amphibious Unit, 22nd, 128
Marine Amphibious Unit (MAU) Service Support Group, 22nd, 128
Marine Brigade, 2nd Marine Division: Belleau Wood battle, 23, 28–29, 30; casualties of, 30; commanding officers of, 25–26; luck of, 27, 30; Meuse-Argonne offensive, 30; performance and discipline of, 30; return home by and disbanding of, 30; sailing accommodations for, 24; units included in, 25–26; World War I campaigns, 25–30
Marine Corps, U.S.: autonomy of, 1–2; birth and birthday of, 1, 4–5; Cactus Air Force operations, 35; connection and relationship to Navy, 1–2; draftees during World War II, 45; duties of Marines, 8–9; enlistees and all-volunteer force, 45; establishment and early days of, 4–10; evolution of, 1–2; First to Fight slogan, 23–24; Guadalcanal campaign losses and casualties, 39; helicopter techniques and uses, 80–81, 86, 88n1; history of, 2; landing operations as mission of, 57; Okinawa campaign and shortened training programs, 46; performance of, 1, 2; readiness for deployment and missions, 2, 23–24, 153; recruitment methods and plans, 7–8; rivalry between Navy and, 2;

standards of excellence of, 2; unconventional characters in, 12; versatility of, 2; World War II casualties and manpower mobilization problems, 45

Marine Division, 1st: amphibious operation in reverse and evacuation, 84–85; amphibious training of, 64; Chosin Reservoir operations, 73–84; Desert Shield/Desert Storm operations, 144, 146, 150; Guadalcanal campaign, 32–40, 90; helicopter techniques and uses, 80–81, 88n1; Inchon landing, 63–67; Inchon landing planning and preparations, 59–61; Korean War, force strength for, 59; Masan, recuperation and training at, 85; Okinawa campaign, 44, 45–46; performance of during Chosin Reservoir operations, 84, 87, 88, 90; replacements in and training activities, 87; Seoul operations, 67–70, 72; training for Pacific campaigns, 32; World War I campaigns, 25, 26, 27

Marine Division, 2nd: breach operations for Desert Shield/Desert Storm, 143, 148–50; breach operations plan for Desert Shield/Desert Storm, 146–48; character and capabilities of, 26–27; combat power and force strength of, 149; commanding officers of, 25–26; gear and supplies for, 144, 146; great attacks of, 26; Guadalcanal campaign, 39; intelligence support for, 150, 151–52; Iraqi forces, first contact with, 146; Kuwait City, drive and entrance to, 150–51; logistical support for, 147, 148; Okinawa campaign, 44, 47; organization of, 24–25; preparations and training for Desert Shield/Desert Storm, 143–44; prisoners taken by, 150; reinforcements for, 145; reserve forces in, 144; rivalry between marines and infantry, 26–27; Soissons offensive, 26, 29–30; training

of, 25, 144, 145–46, 148; Triangle, movement to and training at, 145–46; trucks for moving, 148; World War I campaigns, 25–30; World War I casualties, 27, 30. *See also* Marine Brigade, 2nd Marine Division

Marine Division, 6th, 44

Marine Division, 26th, 25

Marine Expeditionary Brigade, 4th, 143–44

Marine Expeditionary Force, I (I MEF), 144, 146, 147

Marine Regiment, 1st: Chinhung-ni operations, 92, 96; Chosin Reservoir operations, 83–84; Inchon landing operations, 59, 60–61, 66; Seoul operations, 67–70

Marine Regiment, 2nd, 143–44

Marine Regiment, 5th: Chosin Reservoir operations, 75–84; Inchon landing operations, 59, 60–61, 63–65, 66; Seoul operations, 67–70; World War I campaigns, 24, 25–26

Marine Regiment, 6th, 25–26, 143, 144, 148, 149, 150

Marine Regiment, 7th: Chosin Reservoir operations, 73–84; 1st Battalion commander, 94, 97n2; Hill 1304 operations, 92–97, 97nn1–3; Inchon landing operations, 59, 61, 69–70

Marine Regiment, 8th, 143, 144, 149, 150

Marine regimental combat team, 5th (5th RCT), 52–53, 54–55

Marshall, George C., 32

Massachusetts Navy, 4

matchlock firearms, 14, 15

McCalla, Bowman, 17, 19

McColgan, James, 18

McDonald, Wesley, 130

McKee, Hugh W., 15

McNamara, Michael, 15

Medal of Honor, 16, 38

"Meditations" (Aurelius), 162

Metcalf, Joseph, III, 128, 130, 133, 135, 139

SERIES EDITOR

THOMAS J. CUTLER has been serving the U.S. Navy in various capacities for more than fifty years. The author of many articles and books, including several editions of *The Bluejacket's Manual* and *A Sailor's History of the U.S. Navy*, he is currently the director of professional publishing at the Naval Institute Press and Fleet Professor of Strategy and Policy with the Naval War College. He has received the William P. Clements Award for Excellence in Education as military teacher of the year at the U.S. Naval Academy, the Alfred Thayer Mahan Award for Naval Literature, the U.S. Maritime Literature Award, the Naval Institute Press Author of the Year Award, and the Commodore Dudley Knox Lifetime Achievement Award in Naval History.

The Naval Institute Press is the book-publishing arm of the U.S. Naval Institute, a private, nonprofit, membership society for sea service professionals and others who share an interest in naval and maritime affairs. Established in 1873 at the U.S. Naval Academy in Annapolis, Maryland, where its offices remain today, the Naval Institute has members worldwide.

Members of the Naval Institute support the education programs of the society and receive the influential monthly magazine *Proceedings* or the colorful bimonthly magazine *Naval History* and discounts on fine nautical prints and on ship and aircraft photos. They also have access to the transcripts of the Institute's Oral History Program and get discounted admission to any of the Institute-sponsored seminars offered around the country.

The Naval Institute's book-publishing program, begun in 1898 with basic guides to naval practices, has broadened its scope to include books of more general interest. Now the Naval Institute Press publishes about seventy titles each year, ranging from how-to books on boating and navigation to battle histories, biographies, ship and aircraft guides, and novels. Institute members receive significant discounts on the Press' more than eight hundred books in print.

Full-time students are eligible for special half-price membership rates. Life memberships are also available.

For a free catalog describing Naval Institute Press books currently available, and for further information about joining the U.S. Naval Institute, please write to:

Member Services
U.S. NAVAL INSTITUTE
291 Wood Road
Annapolis, MD 21402-5034
Telephone: (800) 233-8764
Fax: (410) 571-1703
Web address: www.usni.org